A Barfield Sampler

A BARFIELD SAMPLER

Poetry and Fiction by Owen Barfield

edited by
Jeanne Clayton Hunter
and
Thomas Kranidas

with an afterword by
Owen Barfield

State University
of New York
Press

The following pieces have been published previously:
"Day," *The Challenge*, February 9, 1923; repr. in *Best Poems of 1923*, ed. Thomas Moult (London: Jonathan Cape, n.d.), pp. 28–29.
Sonnet: "How shall I work that she may not forget," *Art & Love: An Illustrated Anthology of Love Poetry*, selected by Kate Farrell (New York: The Metropolitan Museum of Art, A Bulfinch Press Book, 1990), p. 62.
"The Silent Piano (for E. B.)," *Nine* 2 (May, 1950), 113.
"Sapphics," *Nine* 3 (Dec. 1950), 39.
"Gender," *Nine* 3 (Dec. 1950), 40–41.
"Merman," *The Golden Blade*, 1950, 61.
"The Milkmaid and the Unicorn," *Time & Tide* (Oct. 11, 1952), 1165.
"Mr. Walker," *Anthroposophical Quarterly* 5 (Summer, 1960), 18.
"Meditation," *The Golden Blade* (1971), 71.
Orpheus: A Poetic Drama, ed. by John C. Ulreich, Jr. (West Stockbridge, MA: Lindisfarne Press, 1983).
"Dope," *The Criterion* I (July, 1923), 322–8.
"The Devastated Area," *The New Age* (July 3, 1924), 116–118.
"Mrs. Cadogan" [as by Michael Owen], *New Adelphi* (March, 1928), 233–9.
"Night Operation" was published in two parts in *Towards* in Vol. 2, no. 4 (Fall–Winter, 1983), 10–19, and Vol. 2, no. 5 (Summer–Fall, 1984), 14–21.
Published by
State University of New York Press, Albany

© 1993 State University of New York

Production by Susan Geraghty
Marketing by Bernadette LaManna

Printed in the United States of America

For information, address State University of New York Press,
State University Plaza, Albany, N.Y., 12246

Library of Congress Cataloging in Publication Data
Barfield, Owen, 1898–
    A Barfield sampler : poetry and fiction / by Owen Barfield ;
edited by Jeanne Clayton Hunter and Thomas Kranidas ; with an
afterword by Owen Barfield.
        p.   cm.
    Includes bibliographical references and index.
    ISBN 0-7914-1587-2 (acid-free). — ISBN 0-7914-1588-0 (pbk. : acid
-free)
    I. Hunter, Jeanne Clayton, 1925–   . II. Kranidas, Thomas. 1927–
III. Title.
PR6003.A665A6   1993
821'.912—dc20   92-30926
                                                                         CIP

10 9 8 7 6 5 4 3 2 1

CONTENTS

This volume is dedicated to
Jeffrey Barfield
and in memory of
Maud Barfield
and
Herbert Hunter

INTRODUCTION

The intellectual vision of Owen Barfield, like his life, spans most of the twentieth century. In the acuity and rigor of his analysis, in the breadth of the materials he encompasses, Barfield is unequalled among his contemporaries. Our century, limping to its close in the shrouds of irony and indeterminacy, has worked hard at marginalizing Barfield.[1] And it is true that his audience is relatively small.

But it is an intensely admiring audience, one which responds actively to Barfield's insistent call to rediscover meaning, to recognize and reinvest in the spiritual in the life of man and in nature. There may in fact be something of a cult of Barfield, especially in America, largely (but not exclusively) academic, largely (but by no means wholly) teachers of literature and cultural studies. There is also a smaller, happier group of men and women who have experienced in person the warmth, the wit, the generous humanity of the man. Some of these are students and academics from America and Canada; the luckiest are his friends. This anthology is presented to both of these groups and to a larger audience. To that combined audience we offer a selection of poetry and fiction by a distinguished man of letters, imaginative writing that developed through the years alongside his critical writings, most of which embody those major themes. The virtually unknown pieces we present here reflect the sophistication of a classical education, of practicing literature for seventy-five years, of reading, interpreting, and rediscovering, of reclaiming origins as well as expanding frontiers. Our primary criterion for selection was literary value. Secondarily, we chose pieces that helped expand and illuminate the career and canon of a major thinker, a canon at once various and subtly homogeneous. Barfield's thinking has always been clearly expressed, elegantly honed and unpretentious, even at its most difficult. But the man loves language and revels in its uses. ("Words are my specialty," he says in a recent letter.) He has

1

explored those uses in most of the traditional genres, and some invented forms, with joy, even abandon:

> who's for the open
> Lift of a language
> Laced with verbs, not frightened of consonants, or
> Juxtaposed stressed syllables, fit for breathing,
> Harshly sweet, strong, quantitatively trim, loud,
> Shoutable English? ("Al Fresco")

The exuberant voice of the poet here and in the numerous poems on poetry included herein, enriches his lifelong discussion of "the felt change of consciousness"[2] and the steadily emphasized subject of language in the philosophical works. We hope that our readers will agree with us that these poems and stories and the two prophetic nouvelles expand, illustrate, and challenge the great themes of the major works.

Owen Barfield was born in 1898 into a predominantly secular family. As a child he absorbed the skepticism of his parents, and as a boy observed his mother's ardent feminism with detachment, a detachment that grew later into distaste. Barfield's personal discipline was shaped by this rather rigorous and intellectual family life. (He tells us that he took the hated daily cold baths his mother prescribed into young manhood.) But there are tender and loving portraits too, of his mother in "The Silent Piano" and, more ominously, in "Medusa"; and of his sister, who was partially deaf, in the unpublished novel, *English People*. In that novel, in the character of Janet Trinder, Barfield explores to an unprecedented extent the terrible experience of stammering. His own boyhood stammering sometimes drove him to welcome the idea of death in his sleep rather than facing school the next day. Out of profound experience of language deprivation, Barfield will emerge as the century's philosopher of the Word.

Because we still await a definitive biography, we briefly note here the middle-class upbringing, his attendance at Highgate School (Coleridge was buried in the crypt of the school chapel), and his early emergence as a poet and a boy of letters. His first published poem was "Air-Castles," written while still at school but published in *Punch* when he was nineteen.[3] Highgate also gave him one of the great friendships of his life, with A. C. Harwood, whose brief but elegant memoir gives us intimate touches of the young student who "made no attempt to win favour with the Establishment" but who "was always regarded as an exceptional person . . . . an eager collector of flowers, and a great lover of the stars." We are told too that as a young man Barfield was an excellent gymnast, a serious dancer who once thought of making dancing his career. During the early twenties he met and later married Maud Christian Douie, a talented dancer and designer who had worked and studied with Gordon Craig. Barfield's friends will especially remember Harwood's last sentence: "But all who have known him personally will wish to record also their profound admiration and love for him as a man."[4]

Barfield served in the British Army before entering Wadham College, Oxford, which he attended from 1919 to 1923. While at Wadham, he met C. S. Lewis (who was at University College), and they developed a deep and lasting friendship. That friendship is best described, largely in Barfield's own words, in G. B. Tennyson's *Owen Barfield on C. S. Lewis*.[5] Any Barfield biographer or editor faces a problem with regard to his relationship with the immensely popular Lewis. On the one hand, the friendship provides an entry point to a larger audience for a Barfield whose seriousness is less available than that of his friend; on the other hand, the pairing of the two seems too often to be posed as a paradigm of success and "failure" with an audience. Lewis's books, obviously different in kind, have sold in the tens of millions, and Barfield's—at best—in the tens of thousands over a period of decades. Yet commentators—one thinks immediately of Lionel Adey and R. J. Reilly—who know the work of both men will suggest the subtler tone, the deeper thought of Barfield.[6] We mention this only as a bit of literary history and a factor in the Barfield enigma.

The friendship enriched both men intellectually. The special generosity of both shows in Barfield's comment: "[Lewis] says in *Surprised by Joy* that he believes I influenced him more than he influenced me. If that is true, which I very much doubt, it is because he made it possible."[7] Professionally, the men were separated, with Lewis at Magdalen College, Oxford (1925–54) and later at Cambridge, and Barfield (who never held an English academic position)[8] in London, and for many of his later years in Kent. His was an unusual kind of isolation. The young man of letters of the nineteen twenties met with too little financial success to maintain that career. Despite considerable publication—*The Silver Trumpet* (1925) (a fairy tale written before the mythic fiction of Lewis, Tolkien, and Williams), *History in English Words* (1926), *Poetic Diction* (1928), and numerous poems, stories, and essays and reviews—a career as a self-sustaining writer did not materialize. The extraordinary novel, *English People*, was the test case for Barfield. Initially well received by a German publisher and described in some detail before publication,[9] the novel was never printed and exists now only in an incomplete manuscript version. By the end of 1930, Owen Barfield joined his father's office as solicitor, a profession he practiced for almost thirty years.

The daily pressures of a professional life which one dislikes are described, often quite frighteningly, in many of the poems we print. In his critical works, these pressures are difficult to imagine; in the poetry and fiction they are palpable. Rhythms of obtrusive noise, meaningless repetitions of motions and words, overwhelming congestion, intrusions on the private self, the sense of wasting and waning time—these provide occasions, sometimes elegant, sometimes harsh, for urban despair of the sort we immediately recognize as twentieth century:

> They build in Station Road. A Kango hammer
> Pounds in the scantlings, like a straining heart.
> Drowning the drills' pneumatic stammer,
> Great buses stop and start.

The poem ends darkly:

> Who shouts? A dog snaps. Fret not so
> For silence. It will come. ("Bad Day")

Owen Barfield was experiencing the urban atrocities of noise (to which he was and is unusually sensitive) and congestion, technological intrusions on privacy and human relationships. The relentlessness of his "professional" life, along with other pressures, led him to the verge of a nervous breakdown—a break-down averted, he tells us, by the catharsis of his charming auto-biographical novel, *This Ever Diverse Pair* (1950). In this narrative the musing solicitor is shown in his two faces—Burgeon the poet and Burden the practical man of vocation; this small imbedded lyric suggests how Barfield wittily managed his depression:

Burgeon: The little waves on London River
              Are bombed with light: they flash and quiver
              And laugh and toss back to the Giver
              His shattered shards. They dance their dance.

Burden: I dance my dance too in that station
              To which He called me—litigation
              To gild the tide of fornication,
              Leases, and lusts, and loan-finance.[10]

Barfield's career in law came to an end or nearly so in 1959, following the publication of his acclaimed *Saving the Appearances* two years before.[11] He was soon to embark on another career as a British man of letters.

Sought-after by American universities in the early 1960s and 1970s, he became a visiting scholar, a teaching professor of phi-losophy and religion, language and philosophy, or English and American literature (according to the university). Barfield was also a guest lecturer at various conferences during those de-cades, including conferences focusing on his work at California State, Fullerton, and Baruch College of City University of New York. His last sojourn in America before his retirement from distant traveling was in the spring of 1981, at which time he was a guest lecturer at four American universities in the short stay of a few weeks. It was during these years that Barfield made and kept many friends, some of whom, including students, made visits through the years to his home in Kent, and a few of whom made lengthy summer visits until his departure to East Sussex. A tribute to Barfield's achievements, a session sponsored by *Christianity and Literature* at the 1982 MLA Convention in Los Angeles, brought together many admirers of his books, both old and new. Those familiar with his critical works feel certain, along with R. J. Reilly, that when "the literary history of our time is written and influential critics are discussed, Barfield surely will be mentioned as a matter of course."[12]

Thinking back to the young Barfield of the early 1920s from this vantage point in time, we see that Barfield made right decisions about his literary career. In 1923, with the publication of "Day" in *The Best Poems of 1923* and the acceptance by T. S. Eliot of his first short story "Dope" for publication in *Criterion*,[13] Barfield's literary career looked promising. But even as he recorded the futility of modern life in "Dope," Barfield was finding his larger subject—the recovery of the spirit in man and nature. In a letter to T. S. Eliot in March 1924, he records his decision not to rest in lament:

> I am a little tired of literature which can do nothing but point out ironically that there is nothing much going on but disintegration and decay.[14]

This was a rather bold statement to an author who had published *The Wasteland* two years earlier.

Barfield had in fact burned some very important bridges by the time he was in his mid-twenties. Having made an initial entry into the world of fashionable letters with poetry and prose, he then proclaimed himself a maverick both stylistically and in terms of subject matter. Barfield embraced romanticism at a time when it was widely seen as "spilt religion" (the phrase is T. E. Hulme's).[15] Most significantly, he became an avowed disciple of Rudolf Steiner and a leading member of the Anthroposophical Movement. This commitment to Anthroposophy is profound and central to Barfield's career. It has touched all his mature work and has also been a powerful determinant of the way in which his reputation has been spread and the ways it has been contained or minimized. What follows is a brief introduction to Barfield's central argument on the evolution of consciousness.

In *Romanticism Comes of Age,* the best statement of his debt to Steiner, Barfield writes of his early arrival at "a fairly well considered theory of poetry as a means of cognition":

> without any particular exertion or theorizing on my part, I had had two things strongly impressed on me, firstly, that the poetic or imaginative use of words enhances their meanings and secondly that those enhanced meanings may reveal hitherto unapprehended parts or aspects of reality.[16]

But it was during his serious reading in Steiner in the early 1920s that he came to realize that what he found there bore out his own theory but at a higher level of cognition:

> so far as concerned the particular subject in which I was immersed at the time, that is the histories of verbal meanings and their bearing on the evolution of human consciousness, Steiner had obviously forgotten volumes more than I had ever dreamed of.

It was no "special treatise on semantics or semasiology among his works" that brought such insight, but rather

> it was a matter of stray remarks and casual allusions which showed that some of my most daring and (as I thought) original conclusions were *his* premises. (p. 13)

Moreover, in Steiner's teachings Barfield verified his own thoughts on the evolution of consciousness—a subject at the heart of his philosophy and one from which all else springs. We find this concisely put in his commentary on Steiner's thoughts: "That human consciousness is perpetually evolving was, of course, Steiner's perpetual theme" (p. 72). One might add that the evolution of human consciousness is Barfield's perpetual theme. From his earliest studies in philology he found that language itself is the concrete evidence of this evolution: "language has preserved for us the inner, living history of man's soul. It reveals the evolution of consciousness."[17]

However influential Steiner's teachings were, inspiring Barfield to higher levels of cognition, he remained his own thinker, as Steiner would have wanted.[18] One might say that, through his study of Steiner, Barfield as "Thinking" man came of age. His lifelong dedication has been to restore *meaning* to our very existence and to that of nature. To a book, his purpose is to bring the modern mind to higher levels of thinking and thus to free it from the materialistic literalism that has taken it prisoner (albeit to our own unawareness) and to convince us of the need to change our habits of thinking. Those minds ready for change and unafraid of challenge will find his books useful Baedekers.

One fundamental misconception that Barfield insists we rid ourselves of is the assumption that through the long ages man has always *thought* as we do now, has always *perceived* his world as we do today. This is to misunderstand the past. We are simply another period in history. Ours too will give way to another. C. S. Lewis, in his prefatory tribute to his good friend in *The Allegory of Love*, states that Barfield "taught me not to patronize the past, and has trained me to see the present as itself a period." The all-importance of this lesson for Lewis one gathers from his subsequent remark:

> I desire for myself no higher function than to be one of the instruments whereby his theory and practice in such matters may become more widely effective.[19]

Once we intellectually grasp this we—like Lewis—are already looking at the world differently and questioning our ingrained habits of mind. The medievalists did not *see* their world as we see ours. Theirs was one of wholeness. As Barfield says, it was "more like a garment men wore about them."[20] Ours is one of fragmented individualism and indifference, an age besotted with material possessions. To understand that thinking and perceiving have evolved and will continue to do so is to better understand our place in the evolution of consciousness and why changes in our ways of thinking are necessary to heal our troubled lives and world.

Intrinsic to biological evolution is the evolution of consciousness. Human consciousness, through the vast stretches of time, has evolved from a total immersion in its physical and spiritual environment to our present-day alienation from nature and from the numinous. Then, there was no distinction between itself and the phenomena, between self and not-self. This unselfconscious stage Barfield calls "original participation."[21] When homo sapiens gradually perceived the phenomena (momentarily at the outset) and began to move from the original unselfconsciousness to individuation, language and myth arose.[22] As human beings perceived more and more and named what they perceived, including the numina (considered first to have had a momentary flickering in their dreamlike consciousness), they became more aware of themselves as detached from nature, distinct from the phenomena but not separated. Despite this ever-growing awareness by humans of themselves in relation to the universe, there nonetheless remained a symbiotic relationship. The *Spiritus mundi* still obtained. The old world view still held in varying degrees until the early seventeenth century. What occurred between this long-held view of wholeness and today's view were the philosophy of Rene Descartes—with its separation of mind from matter, of the perceiver from the perceived—and the later Darwinian hypothesis of a mindless evolution of matter.

Equally responsible for the change in thinking, and paralleling Cartesian philosophy, was the rapid advancement of early modern science of which Francis Bacon was the herald. He introduced and developed the inductive method of reasoning and the necessity of experiment as proof:

> Not only did he maintain that knowledge was to be valued for the *power* it gives man over nature. . . . but he practically made success in this aim a part of his definition of knowledge. In other words, not only 'science' but knowledge itself, that is, the only knowledge that is not mere trifling, is, for him—technology.[23]

This revolution in thinking led to a mechanistic view of nature which has turned a living entity into a dead one with its insistence that only the *observable* in nature is important. Like a dead tree, nature has an outside available to empirical data but no inside. We are so used to taking as *fact* this view of nature as merely having a reality *independent* of us that we have all but forgotten its *qualitative* state (a view presently enjoying a certain revival in the books of the biologist Lewis Thomas and of the late anthropologist Loren Eisley). Barfield puts it to us bluntly: either we redress this distortion of truth or we further doom nature and ourselves. There is no doubt in anyone's mind who thinks on it that nature is dying with our help. The evidence is everywhere. Rather than data, intuition and imagination are needed to start to remedy the ills.

Certainly as destructive of holistic and imaginative thinking is the contemporary philosophy, offspring of logical positivism, which claims metaphoric language to be meaningless, since only statements which can be proven by observation or experiment have meaning. Such thinking ensures the death of the imagination—this ageless process of cognition, rooted in the origin of language, and far more indigenous to the human mind than the later development of logical thinking. In a brief discussion on imagination and the inadequacy of (indeed, the fallacy of) scientific inquiry that seeks to make the world knowable through analytic data alone, Barfield closes:

> Only by imagination therefore can the world be known. And what is needed is not only that larger and larger telescopes and more and more sensitive calipers should be constructed, but that the human mind should become increasingly aware of its own creative activity.[24]

What Barfield asks of us is nothing short of a radical switch in our thinking: to see ourselves in a direct creator-relationship with Nature.[25]

Since the adjustment is not easily done, we might get a foothold on such thinking by considering a rainbow. The one in the sky or the one we bring into being by watching the spray of our hose on a sunny day exists because of three necessary components: water, sunlight, and our eyes. Without our eyes, there is no such phenomenon as a rainbow. We participate in its creation, whether we know it or not.

While the rainbow analogy is not difficult to grasp, what is harder is that we—representatives of humankind through the stages of evolution—give nature her forms as well as name them. Consider a tree (to borrow another analogy of Barfield's). Its reality, according to quantum mechanics (one of the great giant steps in the history of physics), is nothing more than an energetic mass of swarming unseen quantum particles! *We* configure that tree. As Barfield put it of himself: "A tree is the outcome of the particles and my vision and my other sense perceptions."[26] In fine, the human mind, from early ages on, has given form to atomic structures, to the phenomena. To more easily grasp this, we might consider that infant stage when a baby first learns (unconsciously) to *focus* its eyes, when the blur of color and motion becomes a solid, seeable form.

But what we should seriously think about is our own devastating creation from atomic particles or from some equally imperceptible base. Unless we start to think of nature as a sharer of our unconscious being and not as something *out there*, we will further our own destruction:

> The possibility of man's avoiding self-destruction depends on his realizing before it is too late that what he let loose over

Hiroshima, after fiddling with its exterior for three centuries like a mechanical toy, was *the forces of his unconscious mind.*[27]

In short, macroscopic nature is man's *unconscious mind.* The cosmic consciousness, which informs all phenomena and from which rose our *waking* consciousness, is by definition nature's inside as well as our inside or, to put it another way, our *unconscious*-ness. We have all but forgotten that nature has a consciousness, albeit unawakened.

However we attempt to change our ways of thinking, to succeed is to restore the necessary wholeness between ourselves and our world. Once we realize that a cosmic consciousness exists, that thinking "permeates the whole world and indeed the whole universe,"[28] that thinking does not originate in the brain but uses that organ to develop and advance the intellect, then we are thinking a transpersonal reality, and in doing so, we will rediscover Meaning itself and restore meaning to our lives and to the life of nature.

One impulse of this anthology is to negate indifference, to present a strenuous, complex argument for meaning in a world seeking—in rhythms ranging from hysteria to despair—some signs of meaning. Owen Barfield's poetry and fiction stand on their own, but they are also rich and attractive vehicles for the dissemination of his ideas about the evolution of consciousness and the recovery of meaning.

Owen Barfield has been writing poetry for seventy-five years. His first published poem, "Air-Castles," appeared in *Punch* in 1917. In the 1920s and 1930s there was a fairly steady publication of lyrics in small journals, most of which were associated with the Anthrosophical Society. There was some recognition, but on the whole, Barfield's poetry received little attention from the general literary public, though it had a small devoted readership among his fellow writers, including C. S. Lewis. Barfield's poetry grew *in the face of* or even *in despite of* the literary climate rather than *in the midst of* it. There is therefore a strong element of irony toward fashion, of defiance even, of positioning on the circumference of poetic practice, which is yet the felt center of poetic vocation for Barfield. In short, of the more than two hundred poems which are preserved, fewer than a quarter have been printed, and those almost exclusively in small journals. Only "Day" was anthologized and received attention from a non-coterie audience. It wasn't until 1983 that the verse drama *Orpheus* was published,[29] even though it had been performed in 1948 and praised by Lewis, who compared its richness of verse forms to *The Shepherd's Calendar*. The long narrative poem, "The Unicorn," and the much longer "Riders on Pegasus" have never been published.[30] The Barfield poetic canon remains unexplored to an extent unusual for a man of his literary influence.

We print here a representative selection of Barfield's verse, spanning forty-five years of creativity. With customary generosity, Mr. Barfield has helped us to choose and to order the poems. The order is not chronological, but readers will recognize thematic groupings, and clearly the first and last poems are thematic signposts. Barfield's great subjects are represented here: the spiritual validity of man in nature, the complexity of human consciousness, the representative—and regenerative—power of human sexuality. But also here are the stresses and erosions of daily life, the heroic stance against compulsory triviality. Here too are vigorous defenses of the English language and its capacities and of a romantic poetic defiantly hurled in the face of a literary establishment described, fairly or unfairly, as desiccated, dour, and self-paralyzed. In the essay, "Poetic License," written as preface to "Riders on Pegasus," Barfield gives us his epitome of modernist poetry, imagined as a wedding photograph capturing:

> the willed inertia of the stolid couple.* . . . This is not to imply that "phrasal" poets are themselves stolid. On the contrary, it took a long preliminary training and, at the crucial moment, a great deal of grouping and focusing and viewfinding to produce precisely the lymphatic photograph now hanging over the mantlepiece in the furnished apartment.[31]

The severity of Barfield's critique of modernism should not obscure the enthusiasm that major literary figures such as

---

* Parodying T. S. Eliot's addiction to what one of his critics had named "phrasal" poetry.

Auden, Bellow, Eliot, and Nemerov have expressed for his thought.[32] Yet the poems on poetry printed here—a substantial group—are evidence of the problematic of Barfield's reputation: here is a heralded man of letters, part of whose *oeuvre* is ignored, if not actually quarantined.

The prose fiction we present here ranges over fifty years—from drawing-room ironies to apocalypse, from three early stories through the *Märchen* which ends the unpublished novel, *English People*, and on to the 1975 novella, "Night Operation." We here note, again briefly, Barfield's initial success with "Dope" and the beginning of a definition of separation from the reigning style in "Mrs. Cadogan" (a story clearly alluding to the Bloomsbury group in less than flattering terms) and "The Devastated Area" (the dark imaginings of an ex-soldier and his inability to communicate the horror of war). "The Rose on the Ash-Heap" is a substantial fiction, even as it is truncated here, complete in itself and yet serving as capstone and climax of *English People*. Its extraordinary vision of the Fun Fair precedes *Brave New World* by at least a year, and another fiction with which it claims comparison, *The Day of the Locust*, by twenty years. "Night Operation" is a revision of "The Rose on the Ash-Heap" in several ways, but brought grimly up-to-date: the nightmare vision of 1930 has become the demi-probability of 1975. We restate our first sentence: Barfield's intellectual vision spans the intellectual vision of the twentieth century, including its darkest corners. But the hope of the saving remnant illuminates all of his portrayals of the human condition.

This collection would not have been possible without the extraordinary cooperation of its source, Owen Barfield. Advisor, co-worker, and inspiration, he gave us generous access to all his papers and printed materials and, most important, access to his continuing wisdom and good sense. His kindness as our host in our long stretches at Orchard View in Kent was matched by geniality and loving warmth, as friend and preeminent good companion. Our researches were intense and pleasurable, divided by our interests. This division of labor is evident in the preceding Introduction. Professor Hunter is responsible for the middle section on Mr. Barfield's philosophy and aesthetic theory; Professor Kranidas is responsible for the opening and closing sections on the biography and the creative work.

We are fortunate in having further debts. Jeffrey Barfield was a gracious co-host at Orchard View and a facilitator of our work over many years. Jane Hipolito was enormously helpful and, with John C. Ulreich, gave encouragement and advice at several critical stages. A stern third reader from SUNY Press gave us good advice and encouragement. Thomas J. J. Altizer has steadily urged us to pursue our project and has offered suggestions, as have Aaron Godfrey and Joseph Pequigney. Irene Greenwood has cheerfully and efficiently prepared the manuscript. As always, her good taste and good sense improve what she touches. Paul Doyle, colleague and friend, has generously prepared the Index for the book. For carrots, coffeecake, and other comforts we give loving thanks to Herb Hunter and Carole Kessner.

NOTES

1.   See for example, George Woodcock, "Romanticism: Studies and Speculations," *The Sewanee Review* 88 (Apr.–June, 1980), 298–307. On page 302, Woodcock characterizes Barfield as "an English eccentric of considerable learning."

2.   *Poetic Diction: A Study in Meaning* (London: Faber and Faber, 1928; reprinted 1952), 48.

3.   "Air-Castles" (unsigned), *Punch* 152 (14 Feb. 1917), 101.

4.   A. C. Harwood, "Owen Barfield," in *Evolution of Consciousness: Studies in Polarity,* ed. by Shirley Sugerman (Middletown, CT: Wesleyan University Press, 1976), 32–33. Barfield's lifelong friendship with Harwood is commemorated in *The Voice of Cecil Harwood: A Miscellany,* ed. by Owen Barfield (London: Rudolf Steiner Press, 1979).

5.   *Owen Barfield on C. S. Lewis,* ed. by G. B. Tennyson (Middletown, CT: Wesleyan University Press, 1989). See also C. S. Lewis, *All My Road Before Me: The Diary of C. S. Lewis 1922–1927,* ed. by Walter Hooper, Foreword by Owen Barfield (San Diego: Harcourt Brace Jovanovich, 1991).

6.   See Lionel Adey's comment in *C. S. Lewis's "Great War" with Owen Barfield* (Victoria: University of Victoria Press, 1978): "That Bar-

field's thought is both more original and more profound I have come to believe while studying these controversies" (122).

7.   *Barfield on Lewis*, 9.

8.   Lewis proposed Barfield as his successor at Magdalen, and the Appointments Committee had approved the nomination. The invitations had already been sent out for the party celebrating his election when the news came that he had been blackballed. The party was held nevertheless.

9.   *Anthroposophical Movement* 7 (August 1931), 133–36.

10.   G. A. L. Burgeon [pseud], *This Ever Diverse Pair* (London: Victor Gollancz, 1950), 39; reprint (London: Floris Classics, 1985).

11.   Owen Barfield, *Saving the Appearances: A Study in Idolatry*, (London: Faber and Faber, 1957).

12.   R. J. Reilly, "A Note on Barfield, Romanticism, and Time," in Sugerman, *op. cit.*, 183.

13.   "Day" was first published in *The Challenge*, Feb. 9, 1923, 46, and reprinted in *The Best Poems of 1923* (London: Jonathan Cape, n.d.). "Dope" was published in *The Criterion* I, (July 1923), 322–28.

14.   For the exchange of letters between Barfield and Eliot, see Thomas Kranidas, "The Defiant Lyricism of Owen Barfield," *VII: An Anglo-American Literary Review* VI, 1985, 23–24.

15.   "Romanticism then, and this is the best definition I can give of it, is spilt religion." T. E. Hulme, in *Speculations*, ed. by Herbert Read (London: Kegan Paul, 1936). Hulme died in 1917, and *Speculations* first appeared in 1924.

16.   Owen Barfield, *Romanticism Comes of Age* (London: Rudolf Steiner Press, 1944; new and augmented edition, 1966), 10. Further citations will be made parenthetically in the text.

17.   Owen Barfield, *History in English Words* (London: Faber and Faber, 3rd reprint, 1969), 14. Over a half-century later, Barfield put it another way: "Language is, more than anything else, the vehicle of human consciousness, and if you want insight into human consciousness and its evolution, you will get it by studying what is going on, and what has been going on, *within* human consciousness, not by studying what goes on outside it." "Two Kinds of Forgetting," *The Nassau Review* IV, 1981, 3.

18.   In his Introduction to D. E. Faulkner Jones, *The English Spirit*, 2nd ed. (London: Rudolf Steiner Press, 1982), Barfield identifies "the stance which Steiner himself wished to see adopted towards his writings. Think my thoughts without believing or disbelieving them; apply them to an area you know well; and see if they illumine it" (xi).

19.   C. S. Lewis, *The Allegory of Love* (London: Oxford University Press, 1935), viii.

20. *Saving the Appearances*, 94.

21. *Ibid.*, Chapter 6.

22. For Ernst Cassirer, "they prepare the soil for the great synthesis from which our mental creations, our unified vision of the cosmos springs." *Language and Myth*, trans. by Susanne Langer (New York: Dover Publication, 1946), 43.

23. *Saving the Appearances*, 55–56.

24. *Poetic Diction*, 28.

25. Analogously, atomic physicists of the disorderly quantum world, have long argued that the observer cannot be separated from the observed. John A. Wheeler puts it succintly:

> Nothing is more important about the quantum principle than this, that it destroys the concept of the world as 'sitting out there', with the observer safely separated from it by a 20 centimeter slab of plate glass. Even to observe so miniscule an object as an electron, he must shatter the glass. He must reach in. He must install his chosen measuring equipment. . . . Moreover, the measurement changes the state of the electron. The universe will never be the same [because it is composed of such unseeable elements, and to change one you affect the whole]. To describe what has happened, one has to cross out that old word 'observer' and put in its place the new word 'participator'. In some strange way the universe is a participatory universe. (Quoted in Fritjof Capra, *The Tao of Physics*, Oxford, England: Fontana/Collins, 1976, 145).

Barfield is no stranger to the new physics, a discipline he cites often in his works and which plays a major role in *Unancestral Voice*. While atomic physicists have found that the mind creates and conditions the micro-world of physics, Barfield has found that the mind creates and conditions the macro-world of our experience. The order of the universe is the order of our own minds, a proposition yet in the thinking stage of the new physics.

26. *Saving the Appearances*, 16–17.

27. *Poetic Diction*, 36.

28. *Romanticism Comes of Age*, 226.

29. *Orpheus: A Poetic Drama*, ed. by John C. Ulreich, Jr. (West Stockbridge, MA: Lindisfarne Press, 1983). Ulreich's Afterword is an important statement on Barfield's work.

30. The Marion E. Wade Collection of Wheaton College in Wheaton, Illinois is the American repository of Barfield material. The "Mother of Pegasus" (original title) typescript is on loan in the collection. An annotated copy of "The Unicorn" is in the possession of Jeanne Clayton Hunter.

31.   "Poetic License," manuscript version; delivered as lecture at SUNY at Stony Brook, October, 1981.

32.   T. S. Eliot praised Barfield early and late. He accepted the early fiction "Dope," was instrumental in the publication of *Saving the Appearances* and wrote a blurb for *Worlds Apart:* "An excursion into seas of thought which are very far from ordinary routes of intellectual shipping." *Worlds Apart: A Dialogue of the Sixties* (Middletown, CT: Wesleyan University Press, 1963). W. H. Auden wrote a Foreword to the revised edition of *History in English Words* (Grand Rapids, MI: Eerdmans, 1967): "It is a privilege to be allowed to recommend a book which is not only a joy to read but also of great moral value as a weapon in the unending battle between civilization and barbarism" (12). Howard Nemerov wrote an Introduction to the 1973 edition of *Poetic Diction* (Middletown, CT: Wesleyan University Press) which includes this statement: "Among the few poets and teachers of my acquaintance who know *Poetic Diction* it has been valued not only as a secret book, but nearly as a sacred one" (1). Saul Bellow, who carried on an intense correspondence with Barfield in the mid- to late seventies, wrote for the jacket of *History, Guilt, and Habit* (Middletown, CT: Wesleyan University Press, 1979): "A clear, powerful thinker, and a subtle one, Mr. Barfield is not an optimist, but he does believe that we can get out of prison—or the madhouse. Once you have recognized, appalled, that you are indeed behind bars you will passionately desire to get out."

Poetry

DAY

Down in the fens of Lincolnshire a bird
Threw up his head and uttered (like some word,
Spoken in hope, that very softly falls
Upon the silence of despair) two calls.
He waited: and innumerable trills
Filled the old darkness . . . .
                Over Malvern Hills
A lark went twittering up into the sky. . . .
One seagull down the cliffs of Anglesley,
Even as the dawn-song of this lark was dying,
Called, and the coast was filled with swooping and
   crying.

   A tiny pool of light that slid and spread
In shoots and runnels over the flat lead
Face of the chill North Sea: then colour came:
The pool of light turned to a pool of flame
That smoked up into a purple and red mass,
Where—like a face behind a darkened glass—
A circle faint out of the dimness grew,
And, flown with the wine of dawn, looked strangely
   through
At island hill-tops rising warm and green
Out of the blind white seas of mist between.
Chiltern and Cotswold's upland grasses glistened,
Colouring the light with dew: the clear air listened.

   Silent He rose out of that dreamy pall
And hung in the blue ether clear and small,
Till, underneath, the hills left dry and bright
Drew closer, and the valleys ran with light. . . .

Silent He rose and arched up over, and soon
The golden languor of the afternoon
Slept over meadows and sheep-dotted downs
And danced upon the pavements of the towns. . . .
Silent He fell, and east to meet the van
Of night the great Welsh mountain-shadows ran,
Rippling over undulating miles
Of English counties. Piles upon deep piles
Of crimson pageantry were slowly heaped
Against the West. Birds sang. The air was steeped
In memory. Dusk flittered like a bat
Down over England, hovered, and then sat
Darkling upon her, till she cast aside
Her twilight vestments, like a calm young bride,
When love himself has broken down his bars,
And spread her bosom to the quiet stars.

SONNET

Once, once, this evening, let me say: I love you!
Now—while I loose all passion and all woe
And shed no more fine tears that will not move you,
Seeing no more your urgent face; for lo!
Your beauty rises from my blood and hovers
Invisible, and broods with hovering wings
And settles, as the soft snow does, and covers
With its own brightness all terrestrial things—
Settles incessantly on earth from heaven
High out of fathomlessly tender blue,
Till by the quenched beam the low cloud is riven
And peace, the crucified, shines glorying through—
    NOW—while love's body stiffens on life's tree—
    Oh Eve! My Soul! My Eyes with which I see!

Amor ed io sì pien di meraviglia,
come chi mai cosa incredibil vide,
miriam costei quand'ella parla o ride,
che sol se stessa e nulla altra simiglia.

Dal bel seren de le tranquille ciglia
sfavillan sì le mie due stelle fide
ch'altro lume non è ch'infiammi e guide
chi d'amar altamente si consiglia.

Qual miracolo è quel, quando tra l'erba
quasi un fior siede! ovver quand'ella preme
col suo candido seno un verde cespo!

Qual dolcezza è ne la stagione acerba
vederla ir sola coi pensier suoi inseme,
tessendo un cerchio a l'oro terso e crespo!

Petrarch, *LeRime*, CLX

When we behold her, Love and I both tremble.
Great, when she speaks or smiles, is our surprise,
Like one who cannot well believe his eyes:
Whom but herself indeed does she resemble?

Hers, from the arc of her clear brow's profound
Serenity, send down the only light—
My steadfast Twins—to kindle and steer right
Each thoughtful will for nobler loving bound.
How beautiful it is, when that white breast,
In early spring, to some green bush is pressed!
Or when she, like a flower, sits on the grass!

O what a miracle beyond believing
To watch her, lost in thought, meander weaving
A garland for that curly shining mass!

LA DAME A LICORNE

All the world's depth and width around her grace
Are shadows—Oh the utmost ends of space
Run inward to her, like her unicorn,
Seeking to sink in her, to be unborn,
Be time's intensity in space's dearth,
All generations' appetite to birth
Caught in one miracle of personhood.
And, since it doth inhabit (this great good
Clothed with the Sun his plenitude of power)
My very heart, imagination's Earth,
How shall my spring not blossom into flower?

SONNET

How shall I work that she may not forget
The wretch to whom her beauty most belongs?
Like an old fisherman, I'll knot a net
Patiently squatting, bending songs to songs.
Like an old fisherman, I'll spread a mesh
Well-stretched and wide, but strengthy to constrain
From last escape the lively flapping flesh
Of the soft carp, her heart, causing no pain.
Well must that heart go darting here and there
Meet this and that, and beat for him and him,
And, seeming to despise my circling snare,
Glittering in sunlight, grey in shadow, swim,
    Lurk, frolic, double, dive, head out to sea—
    Ay, but not free, thou Lovely One, not free!

THE SILENT PIANO
(For E.B.)

Strings, tremble not! That touch,
    Those hands are laid to rest
That loved your keys too much
    To leave them uncaressed.

Bless your beloved voice
   That kindles house to Home:
How sharp above our noise
   The silence from her tomb!

How meekly Music goes
   With none to tell her nay!
How fades, unmarked, the rose
   Of evening to gray!

MICHAELMAS

I have watched the westering Herdsman disappear
Over the shoulder of the heavenly fells,
And now again the dusk is Michaël's
And Perseus and Andromeda are here
And the mute Swan outsoars the hemisphere,
South, above Pegasus. My Diary tells
What locusts, with disgusting mandibles,
Have powdered into Past the dying year.

Proud stars, I do surrender—everywhere
Your streamers flaunt, my line goes reeling back:
I will be quiet: only be you fair:
Call not the slime of your own fortress 'black',
Nor, supine stretched beneath you on the rack,
Eye me for seeking comfort in despair!

BAD DAY

They build in Station Road. A Kango hammer
Pounds in the scantlings, like a straining heart.
   Drowning the drills' pneumatic stammer,
   Great buses stop and start.

And all day long against this island shore,
Plash after plash, accosting, laps the main
   Incessantly. Again my door
   Opens and shuts again.

Till back again, by catacomb, I go;
Homeward on wheels on rails through tunnels drum.
   Who shouts? A dog snaps. Fret not so
   For silence. It will come.

SONG OF THE BAKERLOO

From Kilburn in to Finchley Road
I carried yesterdays for load.

Without alighting at Swiss Cottage,
I bought another mess of pottage.

Without a light in St. John's Wood
I lost the Battle of the Good.

One song it hums, the Bakerloo:—
No more, no more, no more, adieu!

There was no bread in Baker Street.
I lifted high my marching feet

And stumbled onward through the dark
Four thousand times to Regents Park.

It raps and hums, the Bakerloo:—
No more, no more, adieu, adieu!

From Oxford Circus, overhead,
I asked for stones to bake some bread.

They told me—'Change at Piccadilly
'Your Christian names to Willy Nilly!'

It hums and taps, the Bakerloo:—
No more, adieu, adieu, adieu!

I dreamed one in Trafalgar Square
Cried:—'Will you walk out of the air

'By Underground?' At Charing Cross
I woke and wept and knew my loss,

My last defeat, my Waterloo:
No more, no more, of you, of you.

It hums and drums, the Bakerloo:—
Adieu, adieu, adieu, adieu! . . .

THE SONG THEY SING

Siren, siren worm,
Clearer yearly floats the hymn you sing
Over angry waters, heartening.

'Sailor, Sailor-King,
'Fight no more to overtake mistake!
'Peaceful is the memory of wreck.

'Lover, over here
'Wade and lie—be cradled on these rocks—
'Fingers white shall play beneath your locks!'

Siren, siren worm,
Louder daily winds the song you sing,
Welcoming.

FLIRTING

Coiled serpent of old Nilus,
Light sleeper! I marked the way
You stirred softly, un-coiling
In her young, laughter-loving breast,

And reared soundless, as they talked trifles . . .
Ghost-like, where they chattered gay,
Your crest floating to her bright eyes, and
A fork flickered about the jest.

GIRL IN TUBE

Giggler at nothing, blonde suburban bubble,
Office-escape, your wildwood fancy packed
With movies, chromium, face-cream, rubber-trouble,
Technology's first self-conscious artefact,

Thoughtful peruser of the *Daily Mirror*—
How odd that you should stand, to chaps like me,
For weather and openness, and gusty error
Over the hills—that you, my dear, should be

All that is silent, all that's deep and rich
And sleepy upon the cornfield and the down,
Residual *rus in urbe*, God's last ditch,
The touch of nature that redeems the town!

A VISIT TO BEATRICE

Your servant, ma'am, Moll Flanders. I'll be bold
To make myself known to you. I was told
To do so by a friend of ours, my dear,
Soon as she heard that I was coming here—
Said we should find we had a deal in common—
The music-loving, queer, blue-stocking woman.
D'you like her? I do rather. She's so kind!
Something too fond of reading to my mind,
And then that laugh of hers! It bubbles out
Quite as much when no gentleman's about
As when one's looking on. She seems to see
Round us. I wonder if you doubt, like me,
Whether to praise her sense or scorn her folly—
I feel the same about Poll Moxon: Polly
Laughs at her spark, when he becomes a sot
About her, cries 'Don't be an idiot
'But come to quarters!' Now I feel that's wrong;
Let her think what she likes but hold her tongue!
A man in love's not like a man in drink.
Because we know the stuff they think they think
About us isn't true, that doesn't mean
It's nonsense (Marry, my whole life has been
Proof of that). After all, it makes them do
Pretty well what we like (You know that, too).
Take Betsy Hackett now: though sharp and curs't,
She never mocks a doating lover—first
Cuts him some hair to treasure in his locket,
Then goes to bed with him, then picks his pocket
The day she leaves him, throwing in the pox
For keepsake. Well, the last one swore the stocks
Should teach her! But before it came to blows,
She looked unhappy in a way she knows
And—whether you believe't—in half an hour
He'd asked her pardon, begged her for a flower,
Said he was very sorry, knelt and kissed her
Tenderly—you can't call that nothing, Sister,
Now can you? But I ramble on—they say
You managed yours a rather different way.

Tell me about it—I'd be glad to know.
I doubt there isn't all that difference, though:
Tell me!

Beatrice: Your last-named friend, Elizabeth,
Does well and wisely, guarding from light breath
Of mockery those high mysteries profaned
As soon as founded. I, whom God ordained
Their priestess, thank her. I have also smiled
Consciously, I know all you know, my child!
But I was frank: I smiled to free and save
A stubborn spirit—not to chain a slave.
My thought outruns me; I forget that art
Of earthly Rhetoric—Oh, but where to start?
What terms, what order, what conceits to employ?
Do you remember the first time a boy
Beheld you fair—the shock of shamed surprise
That took your heart, remembering his eyes
Later? So light! It clapped its wings and fled
Before you seized your glass and tossed your head?
Fix now that transience—tell it not to go
And in imagination feel it grow
Through all your being, like a wild sweetbriar
Clambering, or builded palace rising higher
With every dusk and dawn—that palace fair
Is the same temple where my mysteries are.
               Demure (you can be) enter! Sit! Be full
Of gazing, listening, dreaming—does't not pull?
Is not the pavement fair beneath my House?
The roof's pleached tracery of carven boughs?
Hark, how sweet muted moans of lutes and viols
Resolve to organ tones that glut those aisles
With thunderous waves: look, where each thick
     embrasure
Pours in, past columns flecked with gules and azure,
Warm sunbeams shafting through cool shadows piled
Like braided tresses . . . I have often smiled,
Reflecting gladly how, if one profane
Our mysteries here again and yet again,
They still may be restored—but *ahi*, the void

If once the temple's self should be destroyed!
I dreamed it was. I saw the very crypt
Yawn to the sky, the gaping aumbry stripped
Of heaped and hard-won treasure:—fancies chaste
Frisking round coif and bodice and slim waist;
Heartstrings tunable to creaks of dresses;
Salutè;* love-at-first-sight tendernesses;
Cool dreams of brow and eyes, dreams light as
    breath—
The Rose ta'en down and on the altar—Death!
Death—and I saw an Age of saucy queans
Staring and tittering over gaunt machines
To speed destruction, and soft air confined
To be let loose again and blast mankind . . .
        Take comfort: here arch smiles are loved,
    here even
Some a degree *too* arch are soon forgiven—
But woe to her, whose meagre rod impairs
The swift, heart-splitting levin of our tears!
Woe to the peevish, whose thin tears are shed
In anger; she shall not be comforted.
Woe to—my voice fails—oh, when Mother Eve
After her Fall, first made pretence to grieve,
To gain her private ends, Earth vomited
And truth ran backward to the fountain-head—
Those—those—my dear, when women's tears are
    feigned,
Sion is made a show and Jordan stained,
And the dear Lord, who donned our weeping flesh,
Is meanly mocked, and crucified afresh!
       Did you too, Sister, somewhere in your heart,
Deep in the carefully-kept-unlit part,
Raise to the twisted mouth the sponge-tipped spear,
With blood on it instead of vinegar—
His Own—and bid him drink it with a sneer?
Oh fools! This kind of pity is so strong
As, not misused, we might have banished wrong

---

* See the *Vita Nuova*.

And hate, and all things hateful, from mankind!
        Give me your hands! Dear Sister, it was kind
To seek me out—and you must go back soon
To that Dark Sphere beneath the doubtful Moon:
Seek out our friend and (if you remember) say,
I have spoken of her with Cecilia
And know what dreary pangs, what wounded soul—
Self-knowledge keeping pace with self-control—
Let in the loves that through her fancy float.
Pray tell her, certain gentlemen of note
Quarrel here—Chaucer and Molière and Arne—
Who first shall hand her in the smooth pavane:
Say—but they beckon now from Lethe's shore—
Kiss me, my darling! Go. And sin no more.

CAN LIGHT BE GOLDEN?

Can light be golden? That can never be,
The well-informed assure us, because light
Is what we see by, never what we see.

But are the well-informed, I wonder, right?
Those painters of the old Italian school
Seem almost to condense it into sight.

I doubt if Cimabue was a fool,
Or faked the background, or the aureole.
Perhaps they worked to some more secret rule

That light observes—not light through Newton's hole
(The force we see by when we are not blind),
But light inbreathed by man's adoring soul.

Can light be golden? Now recall to mind
That seeding whereof Perseus was the flower:
How sad Acrisius' daughter was confined

In Argos long ago—the brazen tower—
Then Zeus, the Light of Day, with godlike stride
Descending on it in a Golden Shower,

Breaching its walls to glorify the bride.
Can light be golden? Now the truth comes clear:
It is, when wonder meets it open-eyed—

As I am to the light that streams from her,
When she at last is near, and these old walls
Invading, overwhelms their prisoner:

The light that, condescending, disenthralls!
For now the pagan myth's inverted: she
(Look up, and see how smilingly it falls!)
The Shower of Gold; I, wondering Danäe.

POLLAIUOLO'S *APOLLO AND DAPHNE*

Day waned: I to the West looked from a summer Down
Far, far over the weald: space was a sea of light:
    Tellus trembled and toned: joy
    Throbbed articulate: low, I heard:—

Daphne! Thessaly-born nymph, whither hasting? Ah,
Daphne, panting at last, limp in Apollo's arms,
    Who but dreaming pursued thee,
    Well foreknowing a timber kiss!

Two vast bachelor arms gripped an amazing Lyre,
Two deep, humorous eyes twinkled across to mine:—
    All this foliage! Oh dear,
    Each dull poet expects a leaf!

PIERO DI COSIMO'S *THE DEATH OF PROCRIS*

'Here blows campion; here centaury, asphodel,
'Eyebright; here is the sea; here shall her foot be
    stayed . . .'
    Spring-heeled, why do you stop short—
    Crouch low over a single rose?

'Light-foot nymphs of desire, flee to my fingertips!
'Haunt these ponderous hands! Placable god of kind,
    'Pan, be gentle and heal this
    Darling pallid among the flowers!'

SONNET

I am much inclined towards a life of ease
And should not scorn to spend my dwindling years
In places where my sort of fancy stirs;
Perched up on ladders in old libraries
With several quartos pouring off my knees . . .
Translating Ariosto into verse . . .
Paddling about among philologers
And Dictionaries and concordances!

There, on some dark oak table, more and more
Voluminous each day, ye should perceive
My Magnum Opus . . . that one which untwists
Their bays from poets who shirk metaphor
And make rich words grow obsolete, and leave
Imagination to Psychiatrists.

THE ANGRY BOFFIN

The angry boffin rose one morning early,
His ears were full of melodies of birds,
The dew upon the college lawn was pearly—
The boffin settled down to study words.

Enlightenment descended on the boffin
Cleanly and simply, like formaldehyde:—
'I see it all,' he said, 'I am a coffin
'That never even had a corpse inside.'

The angry boffin had not any leaning
To histories that tell how words began
But somehow their contemporary meaning
Annoyed him:—'What a piece of work is man!

'He draws from words imaginary stuffin'
'And talks about his "soul" ' (the boffin cried),
'But language—like a boffin is a coffin
'That hasn't even got a corpse inside.'

SAPPHICS

Years ago bright glimpses of fame allured me,
Hosts of intellectual girls, I dreamed, had
Heard of Barfield's thoughts. How the pretty glancers
    Whispered about me!

Mulched with chat my blossoming reputation!
(O salons! O sherry and dinner-jackets!)
Logan Pearsall Smith to the orient gleam
    Lifted an eyebrow.

Hey! the first hours' shooting was good! the dew
  good!
Whirr! the game rose: *Bangs!* from a double barrel,
Bagging J. C. Squire, bringing down, the first shot,
    Desmond MacCarthy!

Soon was noon: I halted, I peered about me:
Gone were those bright birds! Now the day is ending,
Only barn owls, only a pert woodpecker
    Laughs from the coverts,

Laughs at this daft naturalist, his gaiters,
Useless gun, plus fours . . .
                  Disillusioned? hungry?
Strange to me, most strange! as the shadow deepens,
    Energy waxes.

O mad, O intractable mistress, English!
Time-miraculously-annihilating,
Undeserved, unpublished, aloof, astounding
    Comfort of writing!

EMERITUS
(on not trying to publish verse)

Not with contempt I cease to importune, I
Abhorred the complacence of the coterie,
    Upheld the wide world's jurisdiction
      Humbly—or half of me did: the salesman

Outfaced as best he might, with good humour, those
Ubiquitous *No hawkers or circulars!*
       Objective, eschewed false bravado,
       Nor simulated accord with unction.

Incarceration's doom is endurable
Accepted: why knock, if disinclined for it?
       Why risk the old, uncomprehending
       Stare on the face of a friend repeated?

FIFTY-THREE

Now comes the time: shrewd autumn is on to me:
These mists of late September, what augury
       What's past and in store? What accompt, now
       Destiny opens her autumn budget?

Old strains of wars, reined passion, repulses, woes;
Breakdowns—at arm's length poised by tenacity;
       Will (maugre too much, undeflected)
       Paid with collapse of the fibres ruined:

Blown safety-valve—one morning the lump appears:
Fresh air and outdoors blanch to a memory:
       Scene-shifters—hey presto?—the tail's all
       Hospital walls and the reek of ether . . .

Or shroud they harvest, practical, extrovert,
Soft self contained, warm summer collected in
       Dew fallen, rime, crisp like a biscuit,
       Gemmed on the blades in a bright of morning:

Moist underneath, fecund, merry, innocent
Of sultriness, no longer preoccupied,
       No longer introspective—like these
       Quinquagenarian ruminations?

AL FRESCO
(on modern poetry)

Who's for outdoors? Who's had enough of all this?
Hurl a stone to splinter the sealed-up window,
Pierce the stale, accentual froust, the dreary,
      Droned, never-ending,

Sharply flat, sententiously unromantic,
Unctuously startling combinations,
Postured substantival effects—the bleating,
      Follow-my-leader,
Cant of curt, contemplative tropes' detachment!
Half-asleep, chain-smoking . . . among the wine-
      stains
Smart the conversation—but who's for the open
      Lift of a language

Laced with verbs, not frightened of consonants, or
Juxtaposed stressed syllables, fit for breathing,
Harshly sweet, strong, quantitatively trim, loud,
      Shoutable English?

THE QUEEN'S BEAST
(1954)

It may have been a dream: it may have been a
      prophecy:—
The Wilderness between the Wars—
And, on a sort of throne,
A little knot of hollow men, intoning solemn misery
(Not all of them had seen the wars)
Were turning into stone
The Land of Polyhymnia.
The paradise of poetry was flattened out in adjectives
And table-talk and worse.
I walked into the stables,
Where, bowed before a unicorn,
I found a little Englishman unharnessing a Hearse.

He had a teeny-tiny voice:
It whispered 'Betty's Queen again,
'Imagination's green again
'And lifted is the curse.'

ESCAPE

The mind turns, as the night falls, to its own trauma,
    like a room,
Draws curtains and sinks back in a low chair beside
    the fire
Of self-comfort, hums softly word-music deftly made
From its own woe, the world banished . . . Friends,
    lovers, if ever, now
To the rescue! If I call, grimly, known faces before my
    mind,
Hold each a brief moment, not feeling any love,
Will they plot, *will* they join, will they rise silently,
    bearing me,
Like the twelve swans in the old story, the twelve
    brothers, on their wings
Through the window to the wide world, where others
    are and the labourer sings?

YOU'RE WRONG!

'He was never sore: He remained cheery:
    'He chewed weariness, like sugar:
'The brave beggar! His heart burdened
    'Was unhardened.'
                You're wrong, digger!

In a war, when the sharp chances
    Of the splintered senses crash reason,
There's no poison: when the meat's had it,
    There's no adit for a soft intrusion.

FUNERAL ORATION

He showed how failure may outsoar success
(Said the Old Rat, much moved), who, once inside,
At first in order all the exits tried
Nor grew hysterical, nor passionless,
Nor shocked the free with shriek or gleaming tooth,
Nor frothed, nor bit, nor flew into a rage,
Nor dashed in circles round and shook the cage—
And when, with lapse of time, he felt the truth,
How still our brother in the corner sat
And, shamming free, captivity dissembled!
While on his stern face not a whisker trembled!
Oh if, when death proclaimed his Exeat,
He did not mourn, neither shall we today,
My friends, but, standing over him, still say
Proudly to all the world: This was a rat!

MEDUSA

If I had rushed and told you that, while I was
    washing,
        I'd broken the bathroom glass,
Would you have pitied and laughed at my woebegone
    littleness, Mother?
        I was afraid you'd be cross.

If I had mentioned, Beloved, the sky-burnt Gentians
        That bloom far up on the Pass,
Would you have listened with shining eyes, and
    might you have followed?
        I was afraid you'd be cross.

If I had stretched out a hand from my wretched
    pillow
        And rung for you, Nurse,
Would you have bustled in, gripped and manipulated
    the muscle?
        I was afraid you'd be cross.

So I turned my knees to the wall and the easier anger
        In the masculine voice,

And gave up trying to hide those soft parts, where—
   in the Garden—
     I was afraid He'd be cross.

SONG OF ANGER

Long ago, as I remember,
   Loud I often laughed at play—
Anger anger anger anger,
   Anger whipped the laughs away.

Tall I grew: as thought grew stronger,
   Quest was keen and quips were gay:
Time to draw the breath and ponder
Mine no longer—anger, anger,
Anger choked it all away.

Bred a pagan, in His danger,
   Music startled me: one day
I, the gentile, I, the stranger,
Kissed the small one in the manger—
Anger, unrelenting anger,
   Anger wiped the taste away.

So I sought to be a singer,
   Scrawled the leaves with many a lay—
Anger anger anger anger,
   Anger whirled them all away.

HAGAR AND ISHMAEL

I
HAGAR AND ISHMAEL

'I'm *tired*, Mother!'
          'Tired, Child? Will you Sing?'
                   'No. A tale—
'Of *your* telling, this time!'
               'Oh, all mine are stale!'
'No, Mother!'

'Is your head resting? Lean closer to my side!
'Shall I tell—'
                              'Yes!'
        –the old story of the Little Boy who Cried? . . .
        'Well, one morning Other Mother was cross,
        flashing eyes—'
'*One* morning!'
                        'Don't interrupt! Flashing eyes,
'Cheeks flaming, voice stinging sharp through the
        tent,
'Swore Father no peace, unless Mother went
'Forth into the wild ere she was one minute older . . .
'So she went . . .'
                        'Where was Little Boy?'
                                'Perched on her shoulder!'
'Too little to walk?'
                        'No, but sick—like to die—
'Wanned under the slant stroke of a Wife's evil
        eye . . .
        'Many many a long league she trudged, thirsty
        and sore,
'Till the time came at last when—when she *could*
        trudge no more!
'She bowed down, she sank down by a tall cactus'
        side,
'She laid down the little boy (how he cried, cried and
        cried!)
'She gazed here, she gazed there, she ran
        everywhere,
'From Safah to Morwah, plucking out her hair,
'From Morwah to Safah, seven times to and fro—
'Happy heart that never heard a child crying so!

        'She bowed down, she sank down, a lone
        woman dying,
'Slept . . . woke, as the Sky spoke with a Great Voice,
        crying:—

'Take comfort, Hagar! Rejoice, daughter of Eve!
'This is the Spring the Lord made on the Sixth Day, at eve,
'In the half-light!' She stared . . . Oh, the green, grassy
    bank!
'Oh joy, joy, for the little boy!—they drank . . . drank
    . . . drank!
'She bowed down, she sank down by the sweet
    water-well,
'And the grass glistened, as she, tranced, listened to
    kind Gabriel:—
'A wild ass amongst men the Little Boy should be,
'A great nation . . .'
                                'Is that all?'
                                        'Nay, hearken to me:
'The old tale, the same tale, the true story goes
'That oft since, in the half-light, the sweet water flows
'For the stiff neck of a wild ass among men, my dove,
'As an old woman's breast swells with the soft milk of
    love!'

II
THE SPY

So you cry mercy? You can't breathe? You choke?
    Gasp away!
But speak nought, if you prize life, till you've heard all I'll
    say:—
I know—you crept up to the camp (wonderful craft)—
Those still shadows on the dim-lighted tent-wall! you
    laughed:
'Twas too easy! 'Man lying in girl's lap' they said,
Your pleased eyes, and 'The fool's off his guard—
    strike him dead!'

Oh sage Thinker! most circumspect Isaac-man!
Ere you sneak back to your Lord, learn what a Bond-
    woman can!
Let harsh Sarah's seed blossom in swilled, glutted
    swine,

Their eyes, bulging with greed, glued on a fat
    concubine,
Their hair, ripe for the shears, flowing in waves over
    her knees,
Thralls, burdened with lust, itching with Law, melted
    in ease . . .
(D'you hear? Can't you nod? What! Have I limned
    well what it meant
To your mean, sharp little brain, fox, the rune
    scrawled on the tent?)

    When you hear music again, under the harp's
    plaintive string
Hear the battle-yell of a free soul relaxed, ready to
    spring
At a cur's throat or a king's throne on the gad—ready
    to die
Riding forth in the proud-front of its own chivalry.
Set *this* picture against that, when you see shadows
    again:—

    Have you marked, owl, how long shadows walk
    over the plain
At dusk, sliding ahead, seeking a sun fresh from the
    breeze
Of his night-bath in the West lands, the green ocean,
    the trees?
When I dream, plucking the harp, singing her soft
    songs, when I lie
In her arms, such are the far shadows we cast,
    Mother and I—
Long shadows—ghosts—giants—towers—soaring
    away
To where East merges in West, plucking To-morrow
    from To-day . . .

    Be off, son of a dog! See that we're ten paces apart
Ere I count five, or my shaft flies through your—off!
    Off!—through your heart!

III
ISHMAEL

Is the sword drawn? Does the spear stand by
the bed's side? Is he sharp?
Does the sling hang from the carved peg that was
fixed there for the harp?
I will sleep now. I shall sleep easily—ha! Is this I?
Who went whimpering *Hail, brother!*—hoped,
shrinking and shy,
For a kind answer, crept round, like a slave recently
bought,
Ducked, guarded my face, winced and was sad,
wistfully sought
To discern friend from foe (friend? there is no "friend"
for the brave!)
To attain rest from rebuffs (rest? there is no rest but
the grave!)
Who deemed anguish could end never, nor leave
stinging the thong
Of the whip, wept into sleep moaning *How long,
Father, how long?*
      Nor marked, ignorant fool, down in the deep
marrowy part
How the Lord slowly by stealth stiffened a soft Isaac-
heart
That pined ever for love (rather for ease—loathing a
fight)?
I shall spring gladly alert early; for down under the
night,
When I wake now with the dawn, swiftly the vast
weariness drops
Like a leech bloated with blood, leaving me brisk:
whimpering stops:
My brow knits of its own motion: snaps fast in my
breast
The bronze flange of the door shutting off all craving
for rest . . .
'To what end, Mother, what end?' None that I feel.
Only He girds—

Yet—'will make him a great nation!' Yourself quoted
the words.
When the Lord planneth a strong tower, the soil
fiercely he delves:
Every man's hand is against mine—let them watch
out for themselves!

GENDER

None knows the truth; none knows what the answer
is:
Solve—grant a boon not granted to Oedipus,
O mighty, girl-faced, lion-bodied
Sphinx—the unbearable, dark enigma!

Some call it sin, concupiscence, appetite—
Eros defiles true, ghostly communion,
All's greed that transpires through the body,
Love's of the soul, and abhors her earrings;

Why link her arm? Fast fellow, so close to her
Outside a ballroom! (Stoutly the puritans
Affirm a disjunct proposition—
Lust—or the phlegm of desireless friendship)

Some name it 'sex'—dry, Fabian, feminist
Minds, neuter psyches, leftward in politics
Inclined, the guilt-complex repressed—all
Gender for them's to be Freud or *phi* shelves.

Come, come! The truth's plain—*semper*—*ab omnibus*—
Wedlock's the key—*carte blanche*!
Are you sure of it?
Uxorious Victorian mates
Look pretty queer on a page of Patmore!

Well—rule out all that delicate tenderness,
Your tiny hand is cold, and the rest of it—
So! Next you'll unseat inspiration:
Oh, many times, many times the curve of

Her cheek released deep sources of energy . . .
Stop soaring! Concentrate on Policewomen,

Headmistresses, Chars, the Hon. Member
Firm on her feet in the House of Commons:

Do Gender's roots thrust down to the depths of us,
Fling branches up to our cerebral firmament,
         The Tree of Life's high, tiniest twigs
      Tangle with twigs of the Tree of Knowledge?

Or shall we equate now masculine, feminine?
Identical bipeds for all purposes,
         Shall ladies be parsons, be judges?
      Think of her mind: she's a *person*!
                                    Nonsense!

What signifies Eve's brain? She's the universe
Compact in five-foot-six—rather Poetry
         Incarnate—all musical Nature—
      God's manifest in her grace of walking:

Hush! Lucy wakes, fast entering womanhood:
Earth blossoms, old Sol blinks in astonishment,
         Clouds draw apart white plumes—Pacific
      Ocean's asleep in her simple aura.

Wild Gender tames huge Pan to be personal—
Ah, Fancy!—tame, wild Fancy!—be off with you!
         Truth, truth!—will my question be
      answered?
      Aye, when the blood shall have done with beating!

THE MERMAN

A fair maiden sailed forth on the deep sea for to fish,
She laughed loud and she sang loud as the wind
      thrummed in the shrouds
And the same sound, from boats round, of her
      friends, answered her wish,
      And the waves clashed in the deep, dashed on
      the rocks, washed on the shore.

They called out as they trawled, shouting aloud, Hoy!
      for glee

And the fair maiden hauled hard on her catch:
    presently
The small fish and the large fish in the hold heaped
    she did see
        And the waves clashed in the deep, dashed on
    the rocks, sighed on the shore.

Now why, salt young girl fisher, long long do you
    stare,
Then peal out into loud laughter, peel out like bells?
Like a great hulk, ho, flopped, sulking, an old
    Merman there!
        And the waves clashed in the deep, dashed on
    the rocks, washed on the shore.

She's placed knife for a strange guest on the white
    cloth at home,
And the moon waxed, the moon waned, the suns
    rose and fell:
'To my warm couch, old Merman, you ne'er ne'er
    shall come!'
        And the waves clashed in the deep, dashed on
    the rocks, sighed on the shore.

'I storm-bred, in your warm bed knew no lust to be,
'But your home bright with the gold light was a right
    fair country,
'And to drink all of your sweet small treble voice
    mocking me.'
        And the waves clashed in the deep, dashed on
    the rocks, wailed on the shore.

ENLIGHTENMENT

Proud—was I proud? I felt the flaw,
    God knows, in Stoic pride
And watered each enlightened saw
    With laughter's arch aside.

Mere candour forced me to opine,
    Ah, surely not to boast,
Some truth, experience, wisdom mine
    Beyond the reach of most.

So in good faith I judged. Put case
    I erred; is't therefore just
To grind my unpretentious face
    So rudely in the dust?

First, after years of sober toil
    My mind's calm just enough
To disappear in sharp recoil
    From violence's puff!

And then, beneath such bitter blow
    Still faltering, tired with pain,
By joy more startling than that woe
    To be struck down again!

Man's life should move, a shapely whole,
    From leaf to flower and fruit.
Love, music, nature led my soul
    The long Romantic route.

With Socrates I dipped my feet
    In cool Ilissus' wave.
And climbed with Paul the pathway sweet
    That mounts to Friend from Slave.

Two thirds of life I lived, thought, felt
    And more than once I 'died.'
My heart was schooled to freeze and melt
    And rise the other side . . .

Say rather, tucked up in my cot
    I dreamed a long, long dream,
Wherein a phantom day was hot
    And I, poor fool, did seem

To walk beyond my waking ken
    And, open-eyed to share
A Light that lightens grown-up men—
    Too bright for babes to bear;

Say so, for now those dreams are done—
 They too, like smoke, depart
As, softly veiled, the Sun—the Sun
 That wakes and warms the heart

And drives it headlong through the mind—
 Fast pouring I perceive
Through my old nursery window-blind,
 The eyelashes of Eve.

AT A PROMENADE CONCERT

Flute-note and horn went twisting up, to stroke the
 lofty dome,
                And I, on aching feet,
                Stood, not far from the seat
                Where shone my listening Sweet.

She motioned me to change with her—with mute lips
 fashioned *Come!*,
                While those clear eyes expressed
                Dear heart, come now and rest!
                But I scorned that request,

Shaking my head; whereat she flashed fresh signals
 from her face:—
                Then break the rules! she frowned,
                *And sit! Sit on the ground
                At once!* I meekly downed.

Still not content? She, like a seabird, rose across the
 space
                Which did us twain divide
                And sank, in all her pride
                Of youth, at my poor side,

While singing reeds and wheedling strings wept on
 . . . O Double-Bass!
                O Clarinets! *Ohé!* . . .
                How tender-low doth play
                The gentle *Cor Anglais!*

THE MILKMAID AND THE UNICORN

She was striding a-milking, with the cows before her
Straggling and bunching, swaying in a row—
Phoebe, Paradise, Melanie and Jennifer—
Early in the morning. The sun gleamed low

On Melanie the elderly, mugwump Jennifer,
Amiable Paradise. She loved most
Phoebe, the skewbald Guernsey. Phoebe
Shied at the unicorn, the daytime ghost.

Snorting he collected himself from the horizon
And galloped to the zinc pail's cream-white O:
Jennifer and Melanie pretended not to notice:
Milk of Paradise itched to flow.

Moonblind, the milkmaid saw not the unicorn—
Later, by the buttermilk, she heard him speak,
When he shot into the dairy, whinnied *What about
    Philosophy?*
And vanished in the distances a bright, white streak.

Come up Paradise! I'm tired of *being*!
Farewell, Phoebe—for a girl must *know*!
She's kilted her skirts for the flounder through
    bewilderment—
She's off to the place where unicorns grow!

VIDEO MELIORA

Some say the Muse, though formed to please,
    Is vestal and unkissed,
And some write books to show that she's
    A Psychotherapist.

These paint her riding in the storm,
    Dissolving womb-bred strife
By pelting down coherent form
    On broken bits of life;

Those, in the cirrus-mackerel clouds
    Aloof the tempest's reach—

Ethereal Warmth, where Orpheus broods
Over the birth of Speech.

Ladies—I think ye must be two—
And me you both are mocking,
Who love that aery Sylph—and woo
This passionate Blue-stocking!

SONNET

Where can we hope to swim in love's bright wave?
I find no answer, none. It is most true
I might grow rotten, like the rest, be knave
And call it 'karma'—ah, but not for you,
Not you, who so unseal the very rise
Of lovingkindness in my blood, the jet
That crumbles subterranean galleries
From Cyprus' Isle even to Olivet.
Oh never tell my heart that it must choose
Between you and compunction, or decry
Subservience to Law! my Lord the Rose,
He is more terrible than Sinäi:—
      Not bond but free, but graceless made by grace,
      How can I meet your eyes, his dwelling-place?

HOW DOLEFULLY YOU RAKED INTO A BLAZE

How dolefully you raked into a blaze
The complicated ashes in this grate
And fanned them with the handful of brief days
When you were weak and I was fortunate!
They creep into the room, the bitter fogs
That choke the breath and sting the eyes to crying:
Your love was like a heap of cherry logs
      Over coal dying.

Your love was like a truce within a war,
When hunted faces turned upon the sky
No longer twitch, and hungry eyes explore
New benison, a bombless canopy.
Below the stars the ruined houses send

Forgotten lamplight streaming through the curtain
And—best of all—mistake it for the end,
    With Peace certain.

Your love was like a cloister in a town,
Whose airy wall repeats, with dark between,
The glimpse of grey serenity weighed down
And confidently nestling into green.
A furlong off, an everlasting din,
The buses and cacophony go by it:
But somehow all the little square within
    Is so quiet.

Your love was like the visit of a king
To savage places where his people falter.
Your breast was like a seraph's christening
Of Dives' twisted tongue with holy water:
And now again within your candid eyes
The strength is come, and now that all is over—
That you should feel afraid you were unwise!
    Nor a true lover!

SONNET

When the too-muchness of this angry trade
Is thronging toward the Exit from my mind,
And word is brought my words have been obeyed,
When clerks are leaving and the post is signed,
Then first I falter, like one strained to cope
With multiplicity, I pause intent
With vague regard, my hovering fingers grope
About the desk and find no document,
Following an impulse ineffectual,
I raise a book from there and put it back,
I glance from floor to ceiling, wall to wall,
And, lacking nothing, fret for what I lack,
        Till all at once your tall, sweet, pining ghost
        Behind me whispers 'I am what you've lost.'

THE SONG OF PITY
OR
THE COMPASSIONATE SOCIETY
(For pitee renneth sone in gentil herte.
—Chaucer)

Hiya! Wickedness is busted!
Vice is virtue maladjusted!
Once the world was rougher, tougher,
Now no-one must ever suffer,
Shame on brutal antiquity!
In our Everlasting City
Pure compassion's all the fashion
(Velvet hand in velvet glove).
Sing and sing again the ditty:
Pity, pity, pity, pity,
Pretty pity! What a pity
Pity liquidated love!

SPEECH BY A GADARENE CABINET MINISTER

What if the slope be steep and feet be sore?
    Push on! This crisis calls for grit, not greed!
Our plight demands, as I have said before,
    More faith, more work, more sacrifice, more
speed.

Ye are the pilgrims, masters, ye shall be
    The world's example: On, my *Herrenrasse*!
O passi graviora! On, with me!
    Lo! where that New World gleams afar
. . . *Thalassa*!

SONNET

You said, and not as one exaggerating
(Fine words but rather vehement than true),
But ponderingly, but half-meditating,
Like one embarrassed by an insight new,
You said that somehow I was always there
Within you, oh and, if I understood,
You felt—why do I falter to declare
Your very word?—you felt me in your blood.

Since I have heard you say those careful things
A change has tempered my uneasy plight,
A peace; for if imagination brings,
Imagination calms the restless night,
The restless night, the night wherein I rest
Yea, even in your absence in your breast.

THE SONNET AND ITS USES

Poets still choose it: why has it survived?
I think because its form is swift to teach
Even the dullest wit, or most deprived,
That music's latent in the act of speech.
Its liquid motion through its eager stride
That courts at once and disciplines excess,
Exuberance with rigour, flaunted pride,
Demure economies of loveliness . . .

Vain effort—to portray a form of verse
In images! But what if one may dream
A second form tiptoe behind them—*Hers*?
What if I chose the sonnet for my theme,
By mingling both adroitly, to distil
One Essence too too rare for my poor skill?

RUST

Dolorous is the glimpse from the gliding train
Of discarded cans and cars' gearboxes,
The corrugated wrack, and the twisted rods
Curling like whiskers from bonded concrete.
Huge and hideous the heap of scrap—
The joyless acre of jagged jetsam—
Crankshafts and sprockets and rails and cisterns
Furring all into a ferruginous web,
Sinking together into softness . . .
                              Yet rust
On old iron is air's offspring,
Its tender little flowers of bessemer flame
Telling of closer arterial trysts—

When air enters the exhausted lungs,
Kissing carbon and carrying it off,
Blue blood is plenished, blushes into fire!
When the iron enters my angry soul—
When the dolorous blow bites and bruises—
I will change it into rust . . . Mars' roses . . .
May the blowings-through in blast-furnaces,
The blossomings of blood in blessedness of air,
And the fresh spots on the floating spear
In this pale serum a sanguine flame
Of steel kindle—stedfastness of Galahad,
Unbeaten boyhood of Bors de Ganis,
Puissance even of Percival, when Pelles' wound
Was cured by its cause in Carbonek!

IN

Fruit in a blossom
And petals in a seed,
Reeds in a river-bed,
Music in a reed,
Stars in a firmament
Shining in the night,
Sun in a galaxy
And planet in its light,
Bones in the rosy blood
Like land in the sea,
Marrow in a skeleton—
And I in Me.

MR. WALKER

Mr. Walker lies in bed
Every morning, shamming dead,
Till I, returning from a land
Of outward dark and inward light,
Rejoin him—when, at my command,
Mr. Walker stands upright.
But when, as if to be erect

Were insufficient miracle,
Across the floor he carries me
Out to get the morning tea,
What infinite mysteries direct
His locomotion! Who shall tell
With what Pythagorean art
Of space-commuted harmony
He deals to each related part
Proportioned stresses:—*do, re, mi*!
Hear, as above the tray I bend
And straighten, how he takes the weight,
My musical, my lifelong friend
Inaudibly articulate!
So all through yesterday he went
And all my days—my spirit's base,
My soul's precision instrument
To find her bearings here in space:
Left, right, up, down, behind, before . . .
    Ah, let uneasy fools abhor
The bogy man their fancy spies—
That jointed spindle underneath
The blank, imaginary eyes,
Those gaping nostrils, grinning teeth
Mocking and symbolising Death—
Let them abhor!
            But I— But I—
How often in my bath I lie
In Archimedean repose,
Twixt gravity and levity,
And thank, as I uncurl his toes,
The gods who wove this tender skin
And put dear Mr. Walker in!

THE COMING OF WHITSUN

The gentle sunshine threads the trees
And throws bright shadows on the grass
And, glancing down from heaven, sees
The water, where the ripples pass;

But there it breaks to smithereens
And multiplies the lovely day
With leaps and bounds; the hawthorn greens;
    The cherry spray

Is soft with bloom; in how profound
A sea of golden airiness
Her snowy flame is drenched, is drowned . . .
Jesu-Maria! What is this?
The light, the Pentecostal grace
On swell of leaf, in throat of bird!
Many together in one place,
    With one accord,

Being gathered, surely felt it wake,
This talking summer in their blood,
When either what the other spake
Miraculously understood.
Did they then see the forms of names,
As though a word could be a thing—
Or heard they tongues of blazing flames
    Christ-jargoning?

RISEN

Dread not my face. Draw near: Let fan me
    Thy fluttering, fond, unanswered breath!
Life of life, receive the Spirit
    So—from my mouth,
    The Word inwith

Lean near my breast: be all thy solitude
    Soon in the flame it feeds forgot.
Be not afraid of the peace I give—nay,
    Not as the world gave:
    Touch me not!

Seek no caress of my compassion:
    I, who created Behemoth,
Became the phantom of thy beloved
    Charged with ecstacy:
    Touch me not!

WASHING OF FEET

When I bow down before you,
Sweeping the ground to deepen my salaam,
I not so much adore you
As strive to hide my shame:
So like, my brother, to my Lord you are,
So nothing worth I am!

When you do reverence
To this poor, faltering, frail, unquiet creature,
I take for a pretence,
Which gravely mocks your stature,
That ritual act of love: your lowness makes
The height you stoop from greater.

How different may be
Acts that appear the same—what worlds apart
Our inequality
Made equal by your art!
(Yet, when I tell you this, you swear I take
The words out of your heart!)

SACRAMENT

I have taken the bread,
In love, with these others:
Some while it remains
Upheld in the height—
Delaying, in token
Of flesh that was broken,
In the place of the skull
Where dark becomes light.

I have swallowed the wine
That needs no saliva
To meddle it mine
But plunges, a diver

Steepdown in my earth—
From the vault of the brain
To the crypt of the Mothers
The womb of the tomb
Where death becomes birth.

GIZEH

What of the Sphinx? What images of worth, What dreams?
These only: seen first from the side
Almost a great Ship seems to rise and glide
Eastward forever over all the earth
Level beneath it—
From below—before?
O urge me not to babble any more:
That endless, endless gaze above the breast,
That ardour fathomless of azure sky
Carved into speaking silence made of stone.
God's question and man's answer half expressed,
Still couched as though to spring, and still at rest,
Calmly presageful, absolute, alone!

(1981)

BEATITUDE

Blessed are they that do the Father's will
And feel Him not; who think of Him by name
And speak of Him with ease; who, changing still,
Adore Him being evermore the same.
His pulse is slowed to their biography
So long as new disaster breeds endeavour:
Only the lost indwell eternity
And the thought 'Never!'

Blessed are they that live within their lives,
Enduring their identity displayed
Through gentle time; they choose alternatives
And act the spirit out, and plan ahead.
They fill the day with labour, and turn home

At night to gracious warmth and lively greeting:
None but the homeless feel the firelit room
    of the blood, beating.

A MEDITATION

Light in the world—
World in the mind—
Mind in the heart—
Heart in the night.

Pain in the day—
Strength in the pain—
Light in the strength—
World in the light.

FROM *ORPHEUS: A VERSE DRAMA*
Act II (lines 89–259)

[Orpheus is seated beside a glowing fire alone. This scene occurs immediately after Eurydice's death]

Orpheus observes for the first time that he is surrounded by a ring of listening animals.

Encircled by my listeners once again!
Dear creatures, sitting crouching at my feet,   90
Dear friends, who come to help me ease my pain
With your still presence! Say, what can I do?
You have saved me from madness. My pent soul
You have set free, calling it out of prison
Into you on the wings of its own song;   95
What would you have me do in recompense?
How shall I serve you? Answer me!
            They cannot answer me—save with my voice.
It is their bridge. I will sing to them again.
And listen while I sing:

Sings:

Eurydice!   100

Smooth-gliding nymph, bright wife,
Who floated down the river of my life
Clothed in her beauty's seamless vesture
And slipping liquid without pause
From gesture into lovely gesture—   105
Lovely in motion, beautiful in rest—

The Swan

Proud arched above the waters, breast to breast,
I float; in my unearthly whiteness
Gathering the Cloud-gatherer's brightness,
I become Leda's groom   110
And fill with dazzling Helen her dark womb.
I fill with light the light,
But always cruel night
Shoots from my frowning forehead looped to kiss
Itself in the clear water. In cold spite—   115

The Swan & the Serpent, simultaneously

I hiss! I hiss!
You hiss! You hiss!

The Serpent

In your neck's tortuous length
Strives Zeus's sinewy strength.
You become Leda's groom
And fill with Clytaemnestra her dark womb–   120

The Swan

Till at the last
My song is sweet because my life is past.

Orpheus

I hear, O Serpent—and I hear, O Swan!

Sings:

Thine arms about me placed
Melt me in streaming ocean. Mine around thee pressed
Draw down my music spirit to the earth   126
To be the girdle round thy waist—
As ivy round the slender birth-tree clinging—
So we be one flesh, let the spheres cease singing!

The Bull

Stars cease singing—   130
    Music caught
Into body—
    Stamp and snort—

Pulses throb,
    Having new   135
World to fashion,
    Work to do—

Master fear!
    Scarlet warns—
Courage rises—   140
    Lock horns!

Get kind!
    Chew cud!
Thicken muscle,
    Milk and blood.   145

Trust in girth,
    Bones' weight—
Trust in earth—
    Pan is great!

Orpheus

I hear, oh Bull! But yet—   150

The Ass

An invisible warder keeps placing himself in my track!
They are blind—let them whip me! I feel not the lash,
                    let it crack!
No force shall compel me too far! Back! Back!

Orpheus

I hear, oh Ass! Oh obstinately wise!

Sings:

The iron band across my breast was broken   155
    And for a time deep grief was its own balm.
It was evening; 'Orpheus!' my name was spoken;
    'Lift up thine eyes and in the blue find calm!'

The Eagle

I gaze upon the sun. High where I hover
    In the zoned atmosphere he harps and sings   160
Through me, beside me, round me, under and over—
    His word that weaves about me is my wings.

I rise, I drink of that eternal fountain—
    I swoop—Hahee! I am the eagle, I!—
Low in the vale—then high above the mountain,   165
    To lace with living soul the empty sky.

For, when the Father seeks another bearer
    To raise his chalice to his glorious wine,
Some mortal youth becomes a new sky-farer   169
    Caught up on strong wings, and those wings
    are mine!

Orpheus

 I hear, oh Eagle!

Sings:

 One came to meet me
  And soft did greet me,
 A blue-robed goddess
  Out of the night.   175

 Crowned with the stars,
  Her feet on flowers,
 Her dark eyes shining
  With beauty bright.

 And without ceasing   180
  She poured out blessing
 Upon all creatures
  Brought to birth.

 She stilled their needing—

The Lamb

  Peacefully feeding   185
 My close lips wander
  Over the earth,

 Take in her sweetness—
  Then in all meekness
 Give back to man   190
  His Mother's wealth.

 I keep back nothing,
  Give first my clothing
 To part among them
  And last myself.   195

Orpheus

> I hear, oh Lamb!
> You creatures—helpless creatures—I am full of pity,
> Pity for the dumb pain behind your eyes!
> I desire nothing for myself. No! No!
> Nothing for Orpheus. Oh, I am on fire   200
> That burns and scorches not! I thrive upward!
> I could be Semele and not die. Oh Zeus!

The Nightingale

> Tereu! Tereus! Tereus!
>   Philomela! Philomela!
> Of my own vile abuse   205
>   Forlorn bewailer,
>
> Wove in rich tapestry
>   My own sad story,
> Sister, to send to thee,
>   Not for vainglory.   210
>
> A candle clear and small
>   Shows through the night
> By shadows on the wall
>   Its constant light.
>
> So Philomela's song,   215
>   As once her art,
> Is Tereu Tereu, Procne's bitter wrong,
>   Not her own smart.
> Drawn moan and hurrying jets
>   Pour from my tree;   220
> My woe never forgets
>   Procne Procne.

Orpheus

> I hear, oh Nightingale!
> You beasts—oh, you all tell me different things:
> Speak, one of you with more authority;   225
> Which way am I to turn? What shall I do?

The Lion

> Lift up, oh lover, thy heart; let it carry thee
> Manfully over the river of death!
> Stride into Taenarus! Out upon Cerberus!
> Ride on the enemy, rush to the innermost: 230
> Fall at the feet of the seat of Persephone
>   Pour her the gift of thy rhythmical breath!
>
> Lift up, oh lover, thy heart: into Erebus
>   Courage shall carry thee, riding on blood.
> Listen in faith to thy heart—   235

Orpheus

> Oh Lion, cease! You have mistook your man:
> I am not one to wear the lion's skin.
> It is not, and it cannot be, my way.
> Besides, you bid me listen to my heart
> As to an oracle—what folly!   240
> It tells me different things at different times.
> First to stay weeping by my darling's tomb,
> Then to become a priest, and then to seek
> The Maenads in their orgies—why my heart
> Is no more one, one guide, one guardian   245
> Than you have all one voice. Have you one voice?
> Oh then speak out and tell me what to do—
> Oh speak!

All the Animals

> Help us, oh Orpheus!

Orpheus

> How?

All the Animals

> Seek out
> In Hades' realm her whom thou know'st on earth,
> Our mother and our queen, Persephone.   250

Orpheus

> Strange counsel, when I bade you—Oh, I will!
> Eurydice—oh, whither am I led?
> I follow—follow whom? Art thou my friend
> Or my own soul made visible to haunt me?
> I think I am alone . . . Persephone!   255

The fire dies down, as Orpheus rises to his feet, and the animals are no longer visible.

The Nightingale

> Drawn moan and hurrying jets
>   Pour from my tree;
> My woe never forgets
>   Procne Procne.

CURTAIN

CLOSING LINES FROM "RIDERS ON PEGASUS"

One night in June the Palace roses breathed
Such incense, midnight found the royal bed
Vacant; the casement open, where they stood,
Let in soft streams by Philomela shed;
And, welling down from warm stars overhead,
Now faint, now clear, there seemed a far-off
    humming.

Then the Queen whispered, like one in a dream:—
"Hush! Dost thou hear, Beloved? Pegasus is coming!"

And, when the humming ceased, they hearkened
   still,
Motionless, hushed, her cheek against his knees,
To pindrop, garden stirrings . . . out of doors
A separate rustle, like to dawn's first breeze
Or Eleusinian Persephone's
Priest-whispered Name, shivered below their sill;
And they leaned over then, and saw white wings
Moving enough to hold a hovering body still,

And understood the Sending. Soon the night
Quickened to voices flustering, wisps of air
That flashed, like meteors, back, as up they soared:—
Who rides?
       What! Saw ye not the happy pair?
Whither?
      High, circumpolar spaces, bare,
August, await them!
         So, from mortal gaze
They passed and did not pass. Lift up thine eyes,
Reader, now evening darkens on these autumn days;

And dusk itself surprises the clear mind
Conditioned to undying summer eves
And gloaming midnight skies! Lift up thine eyes
Over thy little smoke of burning leaves
And wonder, while thy shaping ghost receives
Huge, ghostly shapes into it! Read, and mark—
Forgetting astro-physics and light-years—
What immemorial Diagrams prick through the dark!

High in the East, beyond those Louvre-pots,
Cassiopeia, the stately, on her chair,
Circles; beside her, toward the Cynosure
Holding her pride true-centred, lest it err,
Honest, broad-shouldered Cepheus whirls; and there
Low in the South, where damp November dims
With rising mist the prospect of deep heaven,
The monster Cetus round the sky's Equator swims;

And what between? What Power upholds the Throne?
What alien Giant, with what sprightly head?
One arm upraised to flash the twinkling mirror,
And one to brandish Herpe's crescent blade,
One shoulder pouring down in a cascade
Swift to his heel that springs from the seven shy stars
Men call the Pleiads—bold—a shower of gold—
Perseus is marching, Perseus is dancing up the wars!

And yet, how still, above Andromeda,
Bending, adores her bridal carcanet's
Enchanting cirque, at Algol in his lap!
While westward, at the star called Alpheratz,
Her dainty foot on Pegasus she sets,
Egging him on, and Pegasus tips gay
And pranceable, and mad, and upside down,
Because he feels the foot of fair Andromeda—

Of fair Andromeda, who in her midst
Holds the great Nebula, that vast maelstrom
Extra-galactic, which the sage proclaim
A furious womb of Firmaments to come . . .
From vain surmise, imagination's way
To Pegasus from Perseus, down those three
Bright steps of flame, which men still name
  Andromeda.

THE END

Prose

DOPE

At 6:30 P.M. the wheels of the factory stopped turning, and five hundred minds, which had been turning with them all day, were set suddenly adrift. One of them belonged to Henry Williams, unskilled labourer, aged twenty, who flowed out through the gates in the long chattering stream and plodded on alone toward his Underground station with nothing particular in his thoughts except a row of the little bright screws he had been sorting all day. "Footbaw Ree-sults!" shouted a newsboy in his ear, and he bought a paper. The little bright screws began to fade, as he stopped under a lamp and read that the Hotspurs had won; then the paper went into his pocket, because you couldn't read walking, and he turned the corner. "*Woman!*" remarked an enormous poster outside a cinema, emphasising the point with a flaming yellow picture of her. "*Because of her Love*," answered the one a little way along on the other side of the street, and "*The Secret of the Sea*." "Mystery Drama"—until a bus stopped panting in front of it and shut it out with "*Pass the Puff!*" "Entirely New Revusical Production" in bright scarlet letters, while the rest of the traffic went grinding by both ways. He was in the queue to the booking office, moving up step by step, staring at crossed threads in the tweed coat in front of him. "Oval." As the ribs streamed up past the gates, he listened to the soothing wail of the lift rising and sustaining its thin note and falling indolently away, then hurried down along on to the platform, where he was pressed safely into place by the man behind and kept there by the woman in front. "Sporty Boyees," he was informed, before the train came in, "are now wearing Swanstripe Pyjamas." Soon he was swaying gently on his strap, as the trousers and skirts of the bright people who ate custard-powder and furnished their houses and appeared on the stage glided faster and faster past the window. Then it darkened. And the endless procession of ribs began again, and he got out his folded paper and held it in one hand, while he read that the King and Queen had sent Caroline Hinkson, of the Almshouses, Pombridge, a telegram of congratulation on reaching her hundredth birthday. But the print was too small, shaking about like that: Paripan, Read *Punch*, P. D. Scotch Whiskey, What does Christ mean to You? Zog it off! Slowly off the platform and along the corridors into another tightly packed lift, where he was raised gently to the surface of the earth. The roar of the street burst on his ears again, as the doors slid back at the top. *"Dewar's"* thundered the sky, and again, more gently, in red "Dewar's" and then half-red and half-green "Dewar's." He walked on towards his own vision of tea and bacon. "J," said someone high up on the left, then "o," then "h," then "n"—"John Bull"; then darkness, then a great shout "John Bull" altogether, and then darkness and soon "J" over again; but *"His Sunday Hat*, Comic," a cinema poster on his right sternly announced. And he turned to watch the rather pretty girl who had just gone by.

But she was hurrying straight on: "I shall say," she thought, "I shall say, 'Look here, Miss Matthews, I may be working under you and all that. But you've got no right'—or, 'But that doesn't mean you've a right to speak to me like that. I'm not going to be the dirt beneath *anybody's* feet!'—then, going right up to her and looking her straight in the eyes: 'So you can just come right off it, see?' " Miss Matthews came off it abjectly, and it happened that Mr. Jenkins was standing near at the time and overheard it all: "Miss Green, I always knew you had more spirit in you than any of the other girls. If you only knew how I admire you—" "Mr. Jenkins, you've no right to speak to a lonely girl like that." "I am sorry, Miss Green, but I did so much want to tell you that I—Hetty!" "Tom!" Hulloa! My! where *had* she got to? No wonder mother called her a lazy, dreaming little fool and wouldn't let her go out alone. "Mother, I haven't been such a bad daughter to you!" "Bad daughter!—you grizzling little—bad daughter, indeed, and what about me? I've been a bad mother, I suppose, slaving all these years, working the skin off my hands!" "Mother darling!" "Hetty!—Oh, Sweetie, Sweetie, and has she been a nasty nagging old mummy, then? Come and—" No. 29. My bus!

Williams watched her mount the bus and jostle up the steps, then he turned and moved on home. He let himself in, trod up the dark stairs to his room, and propped the paper up against the milk-jug before he started in to bolt his tea. "Married Woman has Platonic 'Pal,'" he read in the big headline on the front page. "'Tiny' and 'Biggy?' 'Startling revelations in the Divorce Court to-day.'" He read it, munching, through and began on "Fighting in Ireland: Dublin Man's Story" on the other side of the page. Finished tea, he lit a cigarette and went on with the *Evening Chronicle:* tired of it, picked up *The Boy Bushranger*, which had once possessed a brilliant paper cover, and became engrossed. But in half an hour's time he started yawning and rubbing his eyes. He looked round the room. Well, what was he going to do with to-morrow? He turned to the football page again: nothing worth going to see. What about these "charabangs"? Where did they go to, and how much did it cost? He yawned again and began to undress; in a few minutes his outer garments strewed the floor, the gas was out, and he was in bed behind the table.

Next morning saw him lounging westward in his best clothes. Marble Arch and a long, high motor-car waiting in the sunshine, half full of people. Any room? Yes. Where was it going to? Northampton and back. He didn't quite know where Northampton was or what there might be to do there; but—well—in half an hour's time the suburbs began to thin away, and the dust grew less importunate in his watery eyes, and he felt rather glad he was in his comfortable seat. On they went past rows of workmen's dwellings, past little pink-and-white villas with patches of garden in front of each of them and creosoted fences and wooden gates with fancy names. Long ago the tram-lines had come to a point and ended, and as the traffic, except for an occasional motor, gradually faded from the road, the driver leaned more comfortably over his wheel and sat on, waiting for each corner and hill and village to come up in turn and slide away behind. Behind the last village Northampton was approaching him, and a chat with a man at the garage and the Blue Pig and little Miss Dooley handing out a tall black stout with a white head on it—blast that traction engine! But they got in front of it at last and on and on they rolled, and by went the flat world past Williams sitting in the back. Funny face that bloke had—something like the foreman's—Hulloa! You could walk right off the road there in among those trees, if you wanted to—no hedge or anything.

You'd want to know about botany, though, to get much change
out of that. Out again and over a little common on the top of the
hill. Oo! look at that rabbit—funny little beggar—therehegoes!
On, on, on. Doesn't it make you sleepy? Where's that paper?
"The case was tried before Mr. Justice Maxwell yesterday of
James—" No use, can't read with your hands jerking up and
down like that. Funny shape that cloud is. On, on, on, on.

"Across the road there at 5 o'clock this evening," said the
driver, standing up and turning round in his seat.

Williams climbed down, stretched himself, and decided to
look round for an eating-house. Sitting in his little pew, with a
plate of hot roast beef and plenty of gravy in front of him on the
marble-topped table, he got into conversation with the fat man
in the white apron. No, there wasn't very much to see in
Northampton. The circus went away last week. Had he seen
the Town Hall and the Market-place? So after dinner he wandered along, hands in pockets, whistling sideways through his
teeth, to survey these two attractions. "John Binns," shouted a
hoarding. "Buy your meat from John Binns, and buy it cheap!
John Binns, 16 & 17 Wellington Street, Northampton." And a
cart rattled by with "Family John Binns Butcher" on it. His eye
was caught by the bright sunlit facade of a cinema palace a little
way off. He pottered up to it and stared at the leaning posters.
"Women Men Love" he read in enormous type, and jumped as a
motorcycle immediately behind him started up with two terrific
explosions in the exhaust. "Home is Best" advised the poster on
the other side, a brightly coloured picture of a man and woman
entangled in the telegraph wires. And the clicking wail from
the machine wound soothingly on, as he paid his threepence
and plunged through a plush curtain into utter darkness.

"God bless the Prince of Wales" pounded the piano, who,
on the screen, was tearing through London in an open carriage;
but the scene had changed to Hendon Aerodrome and two tiny
aeroplanes were stunting in the distance high over the massed
black dots that were spectators with upturned faces, and the
huge face of one particular airman was smiling over the whole
screen, and in Chicago a baseball match was going on, while a
bazaar in aid of the Chillingford Orphans' Home was opened
by Lady MacStocker at Maidenhead. But now the big drama
was under way, and shiny-dressed men and women kept driv-

ing up to front doors in motor-cars and running up the steps and going in and coming out of front doors and running down the steps and driving away again. Hulloa! there's something wrong; what's happened? The piano's stopped! He fidgeted and felt in his pockets for a fourth cigarette. Off went the piano again, as he struck the match: "Any time, Any place, Anywhere!" and, "Four more waltzes," thought the pianist, her fingers rollicking steadily on, "will see me through." She saw the kettle on the stove and the teapot waiting in its little green jumper, as her left hand fumbled for Chopin in the pile on top of the piano. Now the whole auditorium was gliding along a country road behind a swaying motor-car with a man lying gagged on the roof—Williams leaned over in his seat, as they turned a corner, and went on watching the hedges flow: "Rather like tiddling along in that old bus," he thought and, when the scene changed, looked at the lighted clock-face at the side and saw that, if he was to get any tea, away he must go.

He was out in the sunlight again. "Footbaw Ree-sults!" shouted a newsboy, and he bought a paper. Then he made straight for the eating-house, had a large cup of tea and several buns, and by a quarter to five was sitting waiting in his place. The passengers gradually collected, and at five past five the driver started up the engine and got in. He looked round: "All in?" and off they went. Slow out of Northampton, then faster, and on and on. The driver settled to his wheel. Williams grew sleepier and sleepier, and saw a little picture of himself having supper and going to bed. On, on, memory unrolling for a moment to acknowledge the particular houses and villages and clumps of trees which it had selected in the morning. On, on, on. What were those nice, smooth little green hills and valleys and patches of sand undulating alongside the road on the left? Oh yes, that was a golf-links—he watched two men trudging with bent heads and bags on shoulders towards a raised grass platform in front of them; but the golf-links dropped behind before they reached it. "That was a fine approach of yours," was saying the tall, thin man in the voluminous knickerbockers, as they walked up to the eighteenth tee, while his heart cried, "If I can get a four here, they'll have to bring my handicap down," and he saw the little white notice in the club-house and his family hearing the news at tea next Saturday.

On, past gaping children and scuttling hens and wagonettes full of red-faced country people, through Little Baldon, down, and up the hill into Muckridge, while on the right the far-away clouds split into long low bars, and the sunk red sun glowed through. Williams wondered vaguely if they had thought it worth while at the factory to let the fires out. Funny colour the trunks of those trees were— Hulloa! another charabanc going the other way. "Hi-i-i!" Now a nice long straight stretch, clear of traffic. Faster. Whoop! —look at that couple on the side of the road! On, on, on, on, on . . .

"Hide me," the man was saying, as he buried his face in her dress, "hide me from the bloody world!"

THE DEVASTATED AREA

He was so tired when he went to bed that he could scarcely find the energy to undress himself. As he bent to brush his teeth, his eyes actually closed, and for a second he tottered back on his heels. At last his head, falling upon the pillow, seemed to draw him gently down into a voluptuous world of black warmth. But when the blind-cord whipped once again against the window-pane, the comfortable waters of Lethe, which had been trembling at his ears, rushed back. Startled, as usual, out of all proportion to the noise, he raised himself in bed to look round the room, and when he again laid his head on the pillow—was wide awake.

For five minutes by the ticking clock he lay perfectly still in the darkness, with his eyes closed, trying not to think; yet he knew no effort of will could conquer that tingling alertness; and now, knowing only too well what it meant and quite powerless to hinder it, he felt his brain starting slowly to revolve like the engine of a great liner; it seemed to gather speed and noise, till it chugged round and round in his head as though it could never stop. He resigned himself to another sleepless night.

So memory began, as usual, to take him backwards through time. But first the loneliness that it had been so easy to stave off all day came softly upon him and settled down round his bed, isolating him from the rest of the world and pointing sardonically to the cold stars that stared through the window whenever the wind blew the curtains. It was a physical sensation too, for he felt the weight of it lying like hunger on his stomach. And then the thoughts—lonely—why was he lonely? Memory insisted on retiring to a distance, and then came mincing back, retracing laboriously all the slow steps of the break with Muriel. Armistice day; the last shot; and the hushed, doubtful little group in the dug-out at 11 o'clock. He is sitting there in uniform, willing for the first time in three years to let his thoughts run on into the future. But they will go back to the past instead: the joy and the agony of that last leave! And now there are to be no more partings, no partings. In one, two, three months at the most, he knows he will be back at home and Muriel in his arms for ever. Great happiness dazes. Sitting there tingling all over with happiness: as if he had had a Turkish bath. He could not sit still any more. He must do something. He had got up and had a whisky and soda.

Early demobilisation: "Good-bye. Good-bye, Old Man!" trying to feel sorry. But he hadn't. The intolerable leave-train; and then the two hours' rush through sunlit Kent in a first-class Pullman. God! what bliss! Victoria Station. Muriel. . . .

The months that followed, with happiness gradually fading away.

He turned over in his bed. Poor Muriel! Of course, it wasn't her fault. He supposed he had been rather a brute—hypersensitive—the war—the—war. How slowly he had perceived the gulf! and she—she had never perceived it at all. Even now she didn't believe it was there. She had imagination, too, and sympathy—(her letters)—he had never met a woman with more. He supposed he never should. Imagination and sympathy and love for him—yet—yet—ah, God! it's no use. Three days in the shell-hole—looking straight into the top of that man's head—he and another fellow. And not even horrified—at the time—they had joked: How are you feeling now, Henry? Top-hole! thank you! . . "Oh, Stephen!" said Muriel, when he told her, "Oh, Stephen!"—just what she had said when little Freddy cut his thumb so deep. Well, what else could she have said? Did he expect her to faint? Yes, but he could still draw a map with his eyes shut of the inside of that head! Oh, what funny patterns!

> "The workings of men's brains. . . ."
> Matthew Arnold.

Now his head began to ache, and every limb, and in the hope of finding forgetfulness he changed his position with two or three St. Vitus jerks.

But no—he is in the Front Line, waiting for the attack. Company Officer. Then the word comes forward that, when the Bosch attacks, the barrage is to drop—where? On our own Front Line! Our own Front Line?—but that's Us! Yes, you give the signal—We drop the barrage. *Dulce et decorum est pro patria mori*. . . . Horror. The sudden black pit of Horror—and the awful nausea! It felt as though his stomach was dropping out in black puddings. Should he tell the men? The sergeants, then? No? My God! I can't keep this to myself! "My dear, how awful," says Muriel, and a little squeeze of the hand. "My dear, how awful," and a squeeze of the hand. Well, what if she did? You bloody fool, what else could she have said? She hadn't been there herself, had she? What else do your men friends say, anyway? Yes, but that wasn't all. She still believed in the British Empire. She never said so, of course. But he could see her thinking it. She believed that on the whole the war was a righteous war—there were profiteers, of course, but no doubt economic causes contributed—but still, on the whole it was a righteous war, and God had fought on the side of the British. Telegraphic address: "Angels, Mons." Poor Muriel! He knew and knew again how much she had suffered during those four years. Then what was the matter? Oh, only that she hadn't been bowled right over and turned inside out, and stamped into the mud; that was all—only that her soul hadn't been disembowelled—only that she had somehow managed to keep her head. I should think so indeed; anyone could have kept his head in England. Well, did he want them all to lose their heads? Oh, I don't know—but that stern, strong philosophy on the lips of people who hadn't been through it—you know!

"Cry aloud for the woe, but let the good prevail." "Cry aloud for the w—," where did that come from? "Cry aloud for _____." He buried his head on the pillow. No, he couldn't get the context. Lord! how that head did ache! But let the good prevail! Oh, yes, let the Good prevail, by all means—Oh, certainly, let the good prevail! "Anyway, Tommy," said Bottomley, trotting out the Prince, "you can't deny that good old God sells the Paper!" And then the Banking Circular—black words on white paper, dancing up and down like midges on a September evening:

> The great debt which Capitalists will see to it is made out of the war must be used as a measure to control the volume of money. . . . To restore to circulation the Government issue of money will be to provide the people with money and therefore seriously affect your individual profits as bankers and lenders. . . .

But that was in the American War. Oh, yes, of course, that was in the American War. That was quite different. This war, said Mr. Lloyd George, like the next war, is a war to end war, and we shall not sheathe the sword until the monster of German Militarism is . . . diddle diddle dumpling, My Son John. What sword? Have you ever felt the edge of one? Have you ever run your finger down the edge of a real bayonet?—no, not the one Peter brought home from Cambrai and we use as a breadknife—I mean a real one. The business end. Let me introduce you—"Mr. Bayonet; Mr. Thomas Atkin's intestines—how do you do! how do you do! Now—twist!—Ow! Ow! Chr-i-st!"

The loud, steady clank, like an ogre's teeth chattering, of the iron bedstead beneath him, and the rattling of all the little ornaments on the mantelpiece told what was left of him that he had a right to ring the bell. They came up and sat on his knees and straightened him out. They sat by him and told him where he was; and when the trembling had nearly stopped, they went away, leaving the light on.

Ah! ah, that was better. Mustn't think about that. "That way, madness lies"—literally. Think of nothing. I'm getting sleepier and sleepier. Nice and warm. In the Mess, Old Canada still talking: droning on and on: women, women, women. Sotto-voce and great big eyes. "My dear Sir, do you really find anything intrinsically humorous in the fact that the human animal reproduces its kind? What—exactly—is the joke, may I ask?" Mustn't say that out loud, of course; but something inside you puts it into words—always in rather pompous, old-fashioned phrases and very long words. Funny! Hulloa, Old Canada off to the clothes-line again? What? don't you know what the clothes-line is, mother dear? Well, you see, on his return from leave each officer is expected to bring with him a—one of the more intimate garments from the wardrobe of a lady friend. *Bon pour les officiers*, what? Oh, be nice, Stephen! Yes, but you see the point is that it makes the Mess so stuffy in the damp weather—like living in a laundry. And besides, you couldn't cross over to the gramophone (they always expect the youngest officer to work the gramophone) without passing through the—the thick of it. Old Canada liked it, of course. "Longing to be in the thick of it." Hulloa! Hulloa! "Longing to be in the thick of it."

"If I know anything of the spirit of the British public schoolboy—and I think I do—there is not one of them here who is not longing to be in the thick of it!"

At school—rehearsing poor old Jameson's funeral service. Eh? Ypres! "On-Ward-Chris-Chan-So-o-ol-je-ers." "Sing up! Sing up!" shouts Captain Benson, right in your ear. "This hymn's got to go! It's got to be heard! Sing up, I can't hear you, sing up!"

(Wee! Steady! hold on tight! No good saying anything—only a boy!)

"'I believe'—now that's the cautionary word: on the word 'God the Father' I want to hear those heels come together with a click!"

No, no, that's not a true story—not even the Sergeant-Major.

And what of the service itself—the ugly little school chapel, the pompous entry of the headmaster in a ballooning gown—rustle, rustle, rustle—mumble, mumble, mumble:

"Do not imagine there is anything incongruous," begins old Luffy from the pulpit (he takes us for Divinity, you know)—"There is nothing incongruous in seeing you here in the garb of war"—(I wonder how he's going to work it round this time)—"Αἴλινόν, αἴλινόν εἰπέ, τὸ δ'εὖ νικάτω. Cry aloud for the woe, says the poet, but let the good prevail!—(We're doing the *Agamemnon* this term)—but let the good prevail!" Did you notice how his voice changed when he said "Let the good prevail!"? Firm, wasn't it? No yielding there, eh? 74 last birthday. Cry aloud for the woe, but don't make too much fuss about it, or you're a mangy little pro-German.

Sitting there, letting it all flow over his head, while he drearily formulates once more the old antithesis between himself and that double row of khaki bodies and pink, contented faces, all believing calmly in football and the British Empire, and the angry old gentleman he imagines they imagine when they bother to think about God.

He leans back in his pew, closes his eyes, and calls up a picture of a congregation of fat German schoolboys stridently announcing themselves as Soldiers of Christ and exhorting each other to gird their armours on (they say there's an understanding among all the big Armament Firms in the different countries—you know, "Cannon fodder")—there was always a certain pleasure to be had from grasping the absurdity of it. Oh, yes, and marching in fours with the O.T.C. past St. Jerome's the other day, he had fancied for a moment that he saw God sitting up on the spire, laughing. It had been quite vivid. He was rather proud of that vision. . . .

"If I know anything of the spirit of the British Public Schoolboy—and I think I do—there is not one of them here who is not longing to be in the thick of it . . . ," comes down in ringing tones from the pulpit. . . . "The grace of our Lord Jesus Christ and the love of God and the fellowship of the Holy Ghost be with us all evermore. Amen. . . ."

Outside. "Now then, you Fellows, double up! Up into the Great School for Lieutenant Boosey's lecture. Double up there!" What's he lecturing on? "The Offensive Spirit." "Training of Platoons, page 11: 'All ranks must be taught that their aim and object is to come to close quarters with the enemy as quickly as possible so as to be able to use the bayonet. This must become a second nature. Remember that a Platoon Commander can best produce the fighting spirit in his men by being blood-thirsty himself, by forever thinking how to kill the enemy, and helping his men to do so. There is nothing like the bayonet. Bayonet fighting produces lust for blood; much may be accomplished in billets in wet weather, as well as out of doors on fine days.'"

Then He laid his head on His right shoulder,
    Seeing death it struck Him nigh—
"The Holy Ghost be with your soul,
    I die, Mother dear, I die."

O the rose, the gentle rose,
    And the fennel that grows so green . . .

"Ow Gawd! I can't stand it. I can't stand it—there ain't nobody kin stand it . . . " "Kick him in the stomach, Sergeant-Major! That's right! Send him forward again." I wish I was like the Sergeant-Major. What is courage? The Sergeant-Major'll yell all right, when the knife's in him. I'm yelling now—like the Red Queen. Imagination. "With stupidity and a sound digestion a man may front much." Shot for Cowardice. Hulloa! Were you one of the Firing-Party? Did you notice the way his knees gave way? What was his mind like? Dreams rushing faster and faster, round and round, like the furious colours on a soap-bubble just before it bursts. Rat swimming madly backwards and forwards in a cage plunged in water, legs kicking, the will to live. "Hi! I must get out of this!" said the rat bursting his lungs. Life is a cart on the way from Newgate Street to Tyburn. I must get out of this. Plenty of people do, you know . . . found with his head in a gas oven. "Poor Boy! Life was too much for him!" Muriel would know he hadn't been callous. A catch in her throat. A catch in my throat—eyes hot. Good Lord! Stop this! Tom Sawyer. (Selfpity Limited.) You baby! Muriel—Muriel! O my darling! "Yes, yes! Poor little Stevy!" No. No use. Well then, write something! Write—write? What's the good of writing? The only people who'll read it are the people who feel it already. The nice gentle people you want to get at, who go on deceiving themselves all their lives, they'll just read the first page and put it away. They'll think you have made a faux pas. Muriel will think you have made a faux

pas. . . . Poor Muriel! Of course it wasn't her fault. He supposed he had been rather a brute—hypersensitive—the war—
the war. How slowly he had perceived the gulf! and she—she
had never perceived it at all. Even now she didn't believe it was
there. She had imagination too, and sympathy—(her letters)—
he had never met a woman with more. He supposed he never
should. . . .

MRS. CADOGAN

When, not so very long ago, a new literary periodical appeared on the bookstalls, boldly announcing its intention of dealing with LIFE, it met, you will remember, with a somewhat varied reception. With the rights and wrongs of this I am not concerned. I only mention it because in the more exclusive circles of intellectual London there was manifested towards that harmless magazine a peculiar kind of dry, almost shocked, contempt in which I happen to be interested. For, being possessed of certain psychic faculties, into the nature of which I need not enter, I was able to trace this subtle, yet quite distinctive emotion to its *fons et origo*.

I have to report, then, that I gradually perceived it radiating in wave-like formation from a certain drawing-room in a residential part of the Metropolis. The vibrations, which were coloured a delicate shade of green, varied in intensity. Sometimes—in the mornings, for instance when the pale yellow curtains had been drawn back and the pale-faced servant-girls were sweeping cigarette-ash from the carpet and carrying stained coffee-cups out to the scullery—they were comparatively feeble. At other times—at night, when the lights blazed down on four hundred square feet of bobbed hair and dinner-jackets—they were often violent. Now the owner of this drawing-room (I am assuming that you are not of her circle) is a certain Mrs. Cadogan, a *blasé* but withal energetic hostess whose evenings are threatening to outshine in restrained brilliance the salons of Maintenon and Scudéry. She is an interesting woman. Her impeccable good taste, which yet does not prevent her from being perfectly outspoken on all manner of subjects, her immunity from the usual prejudices and complexes, her deep underlying hatred of all cant and humbug, and her whimsical attitude towards the clergy endear her to a large circle of discerning friends. Quickly reaching, with care and little luck, a footing intimate enough to allow me to study her character closely, I have been led on by the subject to examine Mrs. Cadogan's antecedents and personal history, and I am now strongly of the opinion that some knowledge of these is necessary, in order to savour the full bouquet of her personality.

Well, then—but, mind you, in the ordinary course I should feel some diffidence over the revelation which I am about to make without her permission. If I feel none in this instance, it is only because I know that in attempting a scientific dissection of my dear friend's personality, I am merely indulging one of her favourite pursuits, while in stressing the influence of heredity, I am actually adopting what I might almost call the "Cadogan convention." Being illegitimate, you see . . .

No, that is *not* the revelation. Mrs. Cadogan makes no bones about that at all. On the contrary, she is never tired of alluding in the most disarming manner to her mamma's little escapade. Just as a conjuror goes on drawing yards and yards of coloured ribbon out of a hat which to the ordinary observer appears to be quite empty, so Mrs. Cadogan continues year after year to extract an endless reel of impish irony from the discrepancy between this early episode in her late mother's career and the moral pretensions of that lady in later life. But more of this anon. Who *was* Mrs. Cadogan's mother? That is the point. I will tell you how I found out.

Those—and their name is legion—who knew the elder lady personally will remember very well a curious habit of hers which I myself used to describe, in cricketing metaphor, as "stone-walling." You know what I mean: you would be talking with her quite pleasantly and candidly upon all sorts of subjects, when it would happen that you—no, not that you actually referred to the forbidden topic, merely that you indicated by the tenor of some innocent remark that you were aware of the *existence* of such a thing. And immediately you would have the vivid sense that the soul of Mrs. Cadogan's mother had been conveyed from her breast, and that in its place there had been erected an eighteen-inch stone wall, from which your remark bounded back, gay as an indiarubber ball, without having made the tiniest impression or the faintest noise. Well, one day I was talking to Mrs. Cadogan, who was in the most excellent form, jesting to me—though she had then only known me for a few weeks—over various intimate memories of her "parent," when from some remark which she happened to drop, the light suddenly began to break upon me. Faintest glimmer of dawn that it was, it yet took me so completely unawares that immediately and as by a kind of reflex action, "O-oh, then," I gaped, like a great booby, "so you were a *Grundy!*"

It was odd that this *gauche* and even impertinent precipitation of mine should have elicited the very token which was to transform surmise into certainty. Almost before I had spoken, the focus of Mrs. Cadogan's eyes had elongated itself till she seemed to be looking at a point several miles behind my head; and between us, if you can believe it, I felt the family stone wall, palpable, forbidding, cold, and certainly not less than eighteen inches thick! Never, as long as I live, shall I forget that moment of illumination.

My curiosity now thoroughly roused, I made a few attempts both on that day and later on to lead up to the subject again, but from the small success I met with, I was obliged to conclude that Mrs. Cadogan *is* complexed after all on one matter—her own maiden name! Thus, I had to ferret out for myself, and not without considerable labour, the interesting facts which follow.

Well, of course, there were stories—there always *are* stories—concerning the identity of the little Victorian Miss's impetuous gallant. With the "single hoof-mark in the soft earth outside the bedroom window" I shall not detain you. But although, of course, this is nonsense, I may as well challenge your credulity at the outset by saying that the psychic powers to which I have already referred made it impossible for me to scorn altogether the notion that Lucifer—not just simply that vague abstraction, "the Devil," mind you; I mean the Luciferic ipseity—him who fell through pride of power—that Lucifer, I say had *something* to do with Mrs. Cadogan's origin. Be that as it may: little Miss (?) was brought up with the Grundy family *as* a Grundy, no distinction whatever being made between herself and Mrs. Grundy's post-marital offspring. In spite of these advantages, however, at the age of nineteen, "the eldest Miss Grundy," as she was called, suddenly vanished from the family circle, where her name was never again allowed to be mentioned.

She reappeared in London at about the beginning of the

century with self-knowledge and a packet of elegant visiting cards marked MRS. CADOGAN. What became of her in the interval, whence is derived her by no means insignificant stock of cash, who Mr. Cadogan is or was—these things nobody knows. It is thought that she had spent most of the time in Paris. For one thing she herself loves to speak of the gay city in such a way as to imply that she knows its social life from within. And there is better evidence. Before he died, the portly and prosperous stepfather had actually said as much to a friend—a rubicund old bachelor whom I have succeeded in running to earth in a boarding-house at Wimbledon. It appears that, as time drew on, leaving its mark on all things, and among them Mrs. Grundy, Mr. G. began to find it necessary to run over to the Continent on business more and more frequently; this had enabled him to keep in touch with his stepdaughter and her friends.

With this I must conclude my references to Mrs. Cadogan's history, from which, as I have already indicated, I have only ventured to lift the veil at all in the hope of throwing a little fresh light on her present character. Nor can I think it has been a waste of time. For myself, at any rate, since making the discovery, how many times, when I have been with the daughter, has some little gesture or trick of speech, some little emphasis or even some little silence, well-nigh deluded me into the belief that it was the mother herself who was sitting there and talking to me! But then the perception of the past in the present has always provided me with one of my keenest delights. To many it may be a matter of indifference. Certainly, when I try to impart a little of this delight to Mrs. Cadogan herself, I do find her unresponsive. I have mentioned her self-knowledge. It is really most odd that in spite of this Delphic possession, my friend is literally incapable of raising to the level of her own consciousness the extent to which her ancestry and early life are responsible for it. It cannot be because of any preconceived notions. If there is a being with an almost religious reverence for the ancient doctrines of Spiritual Heredity and the Environmental Ego, that being is Mrs. Cadogan. Then what is it? Not pride, surely, I once thought. Everything connected with Mrs. Cadogan, her honesty, her chastity, her legitimacy, her own hypothetical soul, her family, her dearest friends—all these things come freely and frequently under the lash of her unsparing wit. At times there is something almost abject in her self-abasement. It is only just on this one little point that she seems to be perfectly unapproachable. Drop but a hint, and there, erected out of nothing in the twinkling of an eye, stands the Great Wall—the Barrier. Not a sound penetrates its granite mass, not a gleam of light. And yet—and yet—in *very* sensitive moods—I have sometimes half fancied that I saw scrawled *across* that Wall, mystical, defiant, in letters of sulphurous flame the proud motto: *"Before Grundy was, I am!"*

But I grow fantastic. Among the other family likenesses I shall adduce Mrs. Cadogan's enclosure from the common lands of conversation of certain proscribed areas into which her friends are not permitted to trespass. Thus, in conversation with her, no word or words must be introduced which seem to her to imply *moral* classification. Naturally this restricts the conversational scope considerably and demands plenty of periphrastic nimbleness from those who have the good fortune to talk with her. The point is, however, that when I am of this number, every time we seem to be getting, as it were, out of bounds, every time some skilful manoeuvre of hers or mine has just landed us back safe but breathless in the midst of the amoral field, I am reminded of those evening conversations with her mother during which the same effort was necessary in order to keep off what one might call the physical or "naked" side of life. For instance, I recollect once quoting before Mrs. Cadogan, in an unwary moment, the remark of a modern critic that "morality colours all language and lends to it the most delicate of its powers of distinction." Believe me, the Wall was up. It was there. Conversation quickly flagged, I left early and observed a few days later that she had added poor Raleigh to—may I call them her *ironicals?* "Earnest" was the epithet with which she henceforward carefully disparaged his name.

Some students of heredity have observed that what is physical in one generation often comes out psychologically in the next, and *vice versa*. The brawny, sub-cerebrated sire, they assure us, begets the weakling with a mighty intellect, and so forth. Whether there is any general truth in this proposition I am not able to pronounce. But I *can* bring forward one piece of evidence in its support; and that is, of course, the case of Mrs.

Cadogan. I think I have mentioned the maternal dislike of overt references to one's physical origin, with its necessarily undignified attendant circumstances? The repetition (only abstracted, spiritualized) of this trait in the daughter is so exact as to be almost grotesque. For if there is one thing which makes Mrs. Cadogan thoroughly uncomfortable, it is a public allusion to her *spiritual* origin. Indeed, she will indulge in all manner of roundabout phraseology in order to imply that she never had anything so crude and clerical. The very phrase sets her nerves screaming—so much so that I feel it is rather unkind even to *write* much more on the subject. Suffice it to say that, as Mrs. Grundy had, for instance, no *legs*—only "limbs," so Mrs. Cadogan had no *soul*—only a "personality." So tender has the lady lately become on these subjects that she is not even sure at the moment whether she cares to admit *that*. But enough. This is hitting below the belt.

I trace yet another resemblance between Mrs. Cadogan and her mother in her attitude towards Social Problems. You remember how the older lady opposed the fitting of safety devices to the little cages in which miners are lowered to their work on the ground that it implied an irreverent distrust in the efficacy of the Everlasting Arms? You laughed sardonically, I expect, when you first heard of this as a young man, but you know now that the attitude was quite logical, based, as it was, on an unshakable conviction anent the impregnable position which is reserved in this world and the next for middle and upper class English bodies and souls. From the same source springs Mrs. Grundy's sturdy refusal to be misled by the insidious endeavours of wild-haired reformers to disentangle the social values from the moral ones. And again, of course, it was this which prevented her from drawing odious comparisons between Mr. Grundy lifting up his voice in church on the Sabbath and the same gentleman voting—but not speaking—against the Factory Acts in Parliament on Monday. But all this is such a very old story. I am sure you are as tired of it as I am. I only ventured to bring it up because this discrepancy between what I might call the Sunday Grundy and the Monday Grundy lives on in Mrs. Cadogan. To take an instance, its subdued radiance may be seen playing over the gulf between her Fabian principles and her passbook, the one so public and the other so very, very private. And if Mrs. Cadogan is in danger—for obvious reasons—of confusing the social values with the moral values, she has proved herself her mother's daughter by discovering a totally new set of values to stir into the great cauldron of snobbery. I mean the aesthetic ones. Call on her one day and get her to talk about Dickens. You will see what I mean.

I could go on for ever drawing these interesting parallels, but I shall content myself instead with making a few observations on two final points: (i) the secret of Mrs. Cadogan and (ii) her influence. Her secret, then, is, in my view, a certain Peter Pannishness. Despite her *blasé* and disillusioned behavior, Mrs. Cadogan has really, at the bottom of her soul, never grown up. All that she says and a good deal of what she does is shaped with secret reference to the haunting wraith of her mamma—and possibly of one or two of her mamma's sisters. Mrs. Cadogan is, in fact, perpetually engaged in shocking invisible aunts. She appears to carry these spectral ladies about with her in her subconscious, very much as wealthy oriental despots used to include certain slaves in their retinue solely for the purpose of having them whipped.* Whence, if it is not from them, does she draw the delicious sense of emancipation and naughtiness which (witness her tone of voice) she still does draw from somewhere every time she quotes from the Old Testament, and *nearly* every time she alludes, let us say, to sexual relations of a kind not sanctioned by that document—relations, mind you, which throughout her adult life, have been the rule rather than the exception in her own circle?

If this is the secret of Mrs. Cadogan, it is still none the less a mystery; and I cannot help asking myself as I contemplate but do not solve it, whether in times to come the little Cadogans will be haunted in the same way by the shades of *their* mamma, and her friends, and, if so, to what manner of life and speech it will lead them. Already, so my journalist friends tell me, there are some doubtful signs of a reaction against Mrs. Cadogan and

---

* The Romans, as every schoolboy knows, even evolved an *active verb*—*vapulare*—which meant "to be beaten." I fancy Mrs. Cadogan's aunts must have created, on the Other Side, an active verb meaning "to be shocked." *C'est leur metier.*

her circle. If this is really so, I am sorry. Personally I like Mrs. Cadogan. I like her for herself, and because I feel the pathos of her biography. Certainly it would sadden me to see, crowning all that she has been through, the last bitterness of superannuation.

Secondly, as to her influence. This, as the reader will no doubt have guessed, is no mean matter. To that little house in Chelsea have resorted for many, many seasons, lawyers, scientists, doctors, artists, scholars, literary men galore, and an endless stream of politicians. The Egeria of literally thousands among the smaller fry of nameless novelists, Mrs. Cadogan can also boast bigger catches. The Apostle of the Unconscious unconsciously drinks influence from her bright eyes. She was the spiritual consort of Victoria's Biographer. The Historian of the World has frequented her drawing-room from a young man, and there is evidence (chiefly internal) that she was at his elbow practically the whole time he was dictating his Magnum Opus. Even the Chronicler of Juan and Joan was once a pretty regular visitor, and some say that it has taken the great man most of his life to shake himself free of her spell. Her hegemony manifests itself in other ways. There are those who met her at an early age and took a violent dislike to her: original spirits, one would think and strong enough to stand alone? Not at all: she frightened them out of their wits, and now it is only from behind the ample skirts of Mother Church that they dare hurl their rotten eggs. It is only in Rome (as the best of them will paradoxically add) that they feel safe in doing as Rome does.

Amid her numerous train of admirers, Mrs. Cadogan's preference is reserved for Literature, her respect for Science. With the former (for she herself has literary aspirations) she feels more or less on equal terms. Before the latter she bows down. No matter what subject is under discussion, the "Authorities" maintain their place unchallenged at her dinner-table, and the regal hostess is not amused by ill-timed jests at their expense. No wonder. These august beings, together with her bankers, form the rock upon which the Church of Mrs. Cadogan's life is built; and none but the totally unimaginative or the very cruel would have the heart to shake her confidence in either.

Yes. On the whole, perhaps, Mrs. Cadogan's influence is the most interesting thing about her. It is a useful exercise, and one which with me has long become a habit, to try and disentangle from each contemporary product of the imagination, as it comes before one, the part of it which is due to her. When, after a little practice, one has acquired some proficiency in the art, the results are positively startling; I had almost said alarming. Really—taking the word "influence" in its broadest sense—I sometimes wonder whether the future literary and social historian of this enlightened age will find very much left but water, when he has precipitated from his solution the protean essence of Mrs. Cadogan.

The two extended prose fictions printed here can be seen as prophetic *nouvelles*, separated by some forty-five years and yet, grimly, a pair. What was futuristic fantasy in 1930 became almost *post hoc* documentary in 1975.

The Märchen "The Rose on the Ash-Heap" is the epilogue of the four-part novel *English People*, Barfield's ambitious treatment of an England which was between the wars and poised on the brink of the dissolution of Empire. Barfield's only lengthy fiction occupied him for several years and became for him a test of his ability to maintain himself as a man of letters. When the manuscript was rejected by several publishers, Owen Barfield became a solicitor. From 1930 onward, writing was technically an avocation.

English People is in foolscap typescript of 550 pages, the original of which is on loan in the Marion Wade Collection of Wheaton College. Unfortunately, pages 78–114 are missing in all known copies. The novel traces the lives of four young English people, very consciously English, consciously transitional. England is pictured as in the midst of crisis; radical ideas clash with traditional, cosmopolitan with national, scientific with religious. The Douglas Credit Scheme is an important issue for discussion, as is a mysterious sense of international "scientistic" conspiracy developing on the Continent, a prefiguration of the totalitarian movements of the twenties and thirties. Most important is the spiritual development of the four main characters largely within the drama of a Church of England threatened by a sense of depletion and fighting for its own identity. Rudolf Steiner is the presiding philosophical genius under the name Brockman, and by the end of the novel Gerald Marston, the figure who appears as a kind of young Owen Barfield, embraces the ideals of Anthroposophy. The Märchen is narrated by Gerald at the end of his quest to the other leading characters. It is a kind of epitome in fantasy of the basic issues of the novel: the dire confrontation of spiritual and materialistic forces, the apparent defeat of spirit in our time and its ultimate triumph.

We have omitted the first part of the Märchen. Earlier, Sultan (the protagonist) journeys from East to West, re-encountering his beloved Lady, the temple-maiden who had fled from the East; the Philosopher and Poet are also characters from earlier stages of the journey. Mr. Barfield's head-note follows.

T. K.

THE ROSE ON THE ASH-HEAP

It is now accepted on nearly all sides that the seeds of destruction were inherent in Western civilization before the War began. It may be that peace will be restored and immediate physical destruction averted. But if so, although some poisonous growths will no doubt have been lopped, the same seeds will still be present with their germinating power unchecked. A terrific shock will have stirred us to the depths and made us watchful, but we dare not assume that it will have made us wise.

If the great heritage of the West is to be preserved, we shall want a new insight, not only to recognize the rotten patches for what they are, instead of welcoming them as triumphs of progress, but also to enable us to penetrate to the core of Western Civilization and draw up its health and goodness to the surface. In the world of the spirit there are shapely things of which our monstrosities are perversions, witnessing to their existence and demonstrating their strength.

The Rose on the Ash-Heap is a "Märchen" between 25,000 and 30,000 words in length. Sultan, the central figure, travels daily further from the East and is eventually lost in a country not unlike the advertisement-machine- and sex-ridden Eur-America which we were getting to know before the War. Formerly ruled and guided by the Lord of Albion, it is now under the total dominion of Abdol, who needs no secret police to enforce his highly centralised authority, since he uses the technique not of scarcity but of plenty—*panem et circenses* in a literal sense.

The story tells of Sultan's many and varied experiences, his encounters, his efforts and his lapses, until at last he finds his way out, not (like some mystics of today) by retracing his steps to the East whence he started forth, but rather by pursuing his westward journey to its utmost limit. There he finds a special master key. This he takes back with him on his final return to the West, where Abdol's blatant and horrible Fun Fair is in progress. It lets him in to the secret Circus under the great ash-heap in its midst. After long and arduous training he himself becomes a circus-rider, is united to the daughter of the Lord of Albion—the bride whom he has so long been seeking—and together with her participates in the apocalyptic end of the Fair and of Abdol's reign.

O. B.

When he had breakfasted next morning and paid his score, Sultan no longer had a penny in his pocket. The whole store of wealth which he had brought with him from Asia had given out. He knew now where he wished to go; but how was he to live? The difficulty resolved itself in an unexpected way. As he was about to leave the hotel, the manager called him aside and presented him with a little metal object.

"A souvenir of your stay in the hotel!" he said. Sultan would have handed it back to him for a worthless toy, but the fellow insisted that he must take it.

"Mr. Abdol's own special orders!" he said. "Everyone who stops here is given one. Of course you can throw it away, when you get outside, if you choose. That's not my affair. But, if you take my advice, you will keep tight hold of it! For if ever you find yourself with empty pockets—you may find it will enable you to support yourself."

"Support myself!" exclaimed Sultan incredulously.

"Yes!" said the hotel-keeper. Just look at it a minute. What would you say it is?" Sultan turned it over in his hand.

"It is a little model of the peninsular," he said, "with Cape Limit at one end and a tiny round hole at the point to represent the hotel."

"Nothing else?" asked the man.

"It seems to be very much the same thing as my friend the Philosopher possessed. A sort of map. Only it is made of steel and his was made of paper!"

"Nothing else?" Sultan shook his head.

"It is a key," said the hotel-keeper.

"Well, I still do not understand how it will support me!"

"In these parts," explained the innkeeper, "the people are growing terribly absent-minded. They seem to lose their heads more and more every day. The result is that there is now scarcely a family which has not somewhere in the house a locked door or drawer, of which the key has been accidentally lost, so that the contents are no longer accessible to them. Now your key is a master-key. I might almost call it the master of masters. I doubt if you will find a lock *anywhere* that it will not open, if you only have a little patience. You understand? People will be grateful. They will pay you!"

"And is it a free gift?" asked Sultan. "I have no money to give you for it."

"Absolutely! A free gift from Mr. Abdol himself."

"Yes. That is just what I find so difficult to understand. I have always looked on Abdol as a hard man."

"So he is, and his gift is hard steel. The very hardest. There is a special process. It will stand anything!"

"But why does he *give* it away?" The innkeeper shrugged his shoulders.

Sultan left the hotel and began, according to the plan which he had formed early in the morning, to retrace his steps exactly over the route by which he had come. The innkeeper was quite right. Although he no longer had any money left out of his own inheritance, he found no difficulty whatever in obtaining a livelihood. The people were delighted with the traveling locksmith, and it was moreover pleasant work; for it was always the drawers containing the things they valued most which they asked him to open. And it would very often happen that they themselves had forgotten how delightful these old possessions were. "I had quite forgotten how lovely it is!" the old women would exclaim, as they drew forth, perhaps their bridal dresses laid carefully away in lavender years and years ago. And on one occasion Sultan left behind him a rubicund, gouty old gentleman playing happily with a toy which he had not seen since he was six years old.

Sultan was particularly surprised to notice that the coin with which his customers paid him was of a new pattern, stamped, not as formerly with the head of the Lord of Albion, but actually with the head of Abdol himself. For fear of offending them, however, he forbore for the time being to ask any questions.

He continued steadily retracing his steps and, as he passed the place of their abode, called in for a few hours on both the Philosopher and the Poet. Both were delighted to see him, congratulated him on his healthy appearance, and—refused to believe that he had been to Cape Limit, or even to Delta! The Philosopher assured him that he had no unopened drawers, though Sultan knew, from his last visit, that this was untrue. As a matter of fact, the Philosopher was so absentminded that he had forgotten the existence of the very drawers, let alone their contents. The latter also assured him with much sly humor that his steel key was *only a copy made from the paper map!* Nevertheless they parted very good friends.

At last Sultan came back to Albion, and in time back to the city of the terrible disaster. He wondered very much if the palace had been rebuilt, what its appearance was and who lived in it; and, although he arrived in the town after dark, made his way immediately towards the centre of the town, where the Palace grounds were situated. Many and great changes had occurred. Where the great wrought-iron gates had stood, dividing the cool and peaceful darkness of the Palace gardens from the garish night life of the town, there was now only a gaudy wooden framework, something like the proscenium of a theatre. This was lit up with a chaotic profusion of parti-coloured electric bulbs, above the top of which stood in enormous illuminated letters the words

FUN FAIR

and beneath, in letters not much smaller,

ABDOL'S GREAT GIFT TO A GREAT NATION.

Inside, it was brighter than day. Strings of electric bulbs were slung to and from posts, dotted here and there about the littered ground, while still taller posts, square monsters of latticed steel, upheld great arc lamps whose carbons, crackling continually, flooded the ground beneath them with a bluish glare. Hammer-blows, shrieks of laughter, the hooting of sirens, an incessant blare of steamorgans, playing different tunes, hoarse voices raised in advertisement and in dispute, all these things combined to fill the air with an indescribable din which made Sultan's heart sink within him, so that he felt he could not go a step further. He looked desperately round him for some more familiar sight. Ah! not far away, a little more softly illuminated than the remainder of the buildings in the fair, stood a large concrete building which bore in tall letters standing up along its roof-ridge the inscription

ABDOL'S PALACE OF DANCING.

Gentle memories began to stir in Sultan's breast; and there was something restful in the lighting of the place which appealed to the tender melancholy they brought with them. He approached the building, and for the first time in his life, he paid money in order to enter a ball-room.

But, once inside, he was glad he had come. No one, it is true, was dancing and there was no music playing, but this could only mean an interval between two numbers. The room itself was dimly yet pleasantly lit with a diffused light, of which the actual source was invisible. The result was a low, romantic twilight, wherein the watery reflections in the highly polished floor moved mysteriously to and fro. Sultan found the subdued illumination very restful to his tired eyes. So low indeed were the lights that it was some little time before he could even see the dancers, who sat, most of them, in little alcoves let into the walls. The alcoves, each of which held a single couple, were shrouded in deep shadow and Sultan observed with pleasure, looming out of the darkness above the heads of each couple, a single red rose. Growing more accustomed to his surroundings, he realised that the couple in the alcove nearest to himself were engaged in conversation. It was the girl who was speaking and, in spite of himself, Sultan overheard her words. She was saying:

"As to what you said just now, if we call the element of intellectual agreement (the psychological minimum datum) x, and the element of pure appetite (the physical minimum datum) y, then we shall have a very fair idea of the meaning of the question-begging term you introduced just now, as it would be when divested of all its accidental historical and emotive accretions. And that I consider to be absolutely necessary before we can even discuss the question!"

"Certainly," replied the man. "When I say, 'I love you,' then, I mean, $x + y$. I mean in the first place that certain specifiable cortical or cuticular—" he suddenly broke off. "Presently!" he added as the two rose to their feet simultaneously. And now Sultan perceived, to his surprise, that what he had at first taken for a rose hanging in the darkness at the back of each alcove was, in fact, nothing else than the two thick lips of an enormous naked negro.* The couple, to which he had been listening, had evidently risen in obedience to the command of their particular negro, who now stepped forth from the alcove and, after first showing his teeth in the broadest of broad grins, began to shoot in and out his lips and his posterior simultaneously, ejaculating, as he did so, in a series of explosive bursts:

> I am de boys
> Dat makes no noise:
> Hoo! Ha!
> Hoo! Ha! Ha!

Meanwhile the man and the girl, standing face to face but without looking at one another, rubbed the front part of their bodies together; after which they turned about and, while the negro repeated his ejaculations, very solemnly rubbed their backs up and down together in the same fashion. The negro then retired to the back of the alcove and the couple resumed their sitting out. Whereupon Sultan heard the girl say:

"The music is getting much better, dear. That was an awfully jolly one." To which the man began to reply:

"—Certain specifiable cuticular reactions would, given the requisite spatial proximity, undoubtedly be effectuated. In the second place I mean to imply . . . "

But by this time Sultan had moved out of earshot. And after finally satisfying himself that the whole ball was indeed no more than a collection of independent performances of this kind executed by the various couples in accordance with the caprices of their negros, he hurried out of the building by the way he had come.

He began to explore the rest of the Fair. Never in all his travels had he seen such indescribable confusion or heard such an extraordinary racket. Crowds thronged everywhere. Men, women and children jostled one another incessantly and all the more violently owing to the vacant mood in which they were wandering to and fro, uncertain whither to turn next. Sometimes a man or a child would be knocked over and nearly

---

* Mr. Barfield now asks the reader to remember that this passage was written "in the unregenerate days before 1930." This passage does not represent his personal view then or now.

trampled by the aimless crowd; but after a time he would get up on his feet again and go on staring and staring without ever having so much as closed his stupid gaping mouth. Every available inch of the ground was filled with gaudily coloured and brilliantly lit Amusement erections. These were of the most varied description. Sultan noticed first of all the huge Roundabouts. They seemed to be everywhere; and they were no longer of the old-fashioned type fitted with rising and falling wooden horses. Instead of these, great undulating green and purple dragons, their backs painted with spots and their carven faces tortured into every variety of fury, terror and amazement, tore round and round, snorting coloured fires from their nostrils and carrying in their open bellies placid, unsmiling rows of chewing and smoking humanity. There were moreover Watershoots, Switchbacks, Mountain Railways, Witching Waves, Cranes, Towers, Great Wheels, Weighing Machines, Slipping the Slip, Looping the Loop—devices for hoisting, lowering or shoving the human body about in every conceivable direction, at every conceivable speed, devices for giving it every imaginable kind of sensation. In one part of the Fair there stood rows and rows of stereoscopic peepshows, through which, for the payment of a trifling sum, men and women alike could gaze their fill upon the most cunningly devised pornograms. The rows were double, one for the men and one for the women, who stood back to back on the series of little platforms which had been fixed in front of the stereoscopes. The more virile and full-blooded type of customer was then enticed further on, by a large notice which hung, beyond the last of the stereoscopes, over a long row of contained booths, bearing the mysterious inscription:

ABDOL'S AUTOMATIC TARTS

Each one of these booths, so Sultan discovered, contained an artifically constructed, electrically warmed lay-figure covered over with real human hair and with splendidly smooth human flesh, which had been obtained by a special process from adolescent corpses. The nude automatons were moreover capable of uttering, through a microphone cunningly concealed in the skull, a few simple endearments! They were of both sexes.

Outside each booth stood an attendant, an elegant young woman smartly dressed in a masculine uniform with a commissionaire's peaked cap and striped trousers, who invited the customers, took their money, and then watched them contemptuously in. Sultan was surprised to see how natural the uniforms looked on these girls, until he learnt that they all came from a part of the land where it was now compulsory, as a prophylactic measure against a certain horrible disease, for all females to have their breasts amputated at the age of fourteen.

The insides of these booths, admittance to which was a little more expensive, were very sumptuously appointed; everything was so efficiently disposed that many customers did not even bother between entering and leaving, to take their cigarettes out of their mouths. Indeed an automatic machine for delivering cigarettes stood beside each automatic tart. There appeared also to be a certain amount of competition between the individual booths, which were numbered; for many of the attendants had hung up outside their curtains fetching placards, in order to attract customers to their own booth. The placards bore such legends as:

SOCRATES SAID DESIRE IS PAIN!
SWAT THAT CASTRATION COMPLEX!
COME ALONG! OED! MUMMY'S WAITING!

and so forth.

Somewhere or other, either in large letters or in small, printed on the placards, illuminated below the signs, stamped on the metal, the woodwork, or the upholstery, the name of *Abdol* was always to be found. Everything was Abdol's. And indeed, apart from the appointments of the Fair itself, there were huge advertisements everywhere of Abdol's proprietary monopolies. Sultan was positively amazed at their number and variety.

It seemed in some ways such a short time since he had been in Albion before, and already the place was hardly recognizable. For instance, right in the middle of the whole Fair, dominating all the illuminated signs over the Amusement Apparatus and all the other advertisements as well, there arose one single enormous hoarding, bearing a fabulously expensive advertisement of Abdol's last and favourite monopoly. Or perhaps it was not yet quite a monopoly. Just before he left Sultan stood and watched its illuminated mechanical changes through a complete cycle. A human figure, outlined in innumerable electric bulbs, hung on a large cross, picked out of the darkness in the same way. For a few seconds nothing changed, but then, in the darkness underneath, the helmeted figure of a soldier suddenly appeared. A line of lights, kindling one by one, ran up like a caterpillar out of the soldier's hands into the face of the figure on the cross. There was another pause, and then, at the upper end of the long straight line, something like a sponge materialised itself. With four or five grotesque jerks, the figure on the cross shook its head to and fro, as if in refusal. There was another pause. Above the cross a great capital "I" appeared, and following it, at some distance on the right, an "N". And then, after a slightly longer pause than before, the whole inscription completed itself unexpectedly in a single flash:

IT'S NOT ABDOL'S

and a second later the entire sign blotted itself out and on the darkness which it left was written a single inscription in letters thirty feet high:

ABDOL'S VINEGAR!

Sultan had intended to seek out the exact spot in these transformed gardens where the Palace had formerly stood. But he now found that he was tired out, so tired that he could scarcely move another step. He left the Fair, therefore, and without much difficulty, though at the cost of much weary tramping, found out the inn in which he had slept the last time he was in the city and in which he had had the hideous dream and still more hideous awakening. Mine Host was as communicative as ever. Before Sultan retired to bed that night he had learnt most of what had happened in Albion since his departure. It seemed that the hotelkeeper had been quite mistaken in his estimate of Abdol's character. Of late Abdol had been positively *loading* the people with kindness!

"How did he begin?" asked Sultan.

"At his instigation," replied Mine Host, "and under his guidance, they took the opportunity of the great conflagration to abolish monarchy and establish the present republic, which is governed by representatives of the people elected by the votes of every citizen over eight years of age. Now, at the very first election, acting on the advice of a popular journal called *The Lollipop*, the new electors unanimously returned Abdol himself as President of the Republic and First Lord of the Treasury in perpetuity. Abdol generously responded by refusing to foreclose on his mortgages on the Palace Gardens, presenting them instead to the nation for use as an Amusement Park for ever. Not content with this, he announced shortly afterwards that, owing to the great wisdom which the nation had shown in combining the two offices of President and Treasury-Lord and, he would add, in vesting the functions of that joint office in himself, he now felt able to revise the whole system under which labour was employed in his factories—which was tantamount to saying the system under which labour was employed throughout the country—practically throughout the world. Mr. Abdol then let the nation into a secret. Engines had long ago been invented, he explained, of such efficiency that, in the bulk of his factories, they could replace some two thirds of the human labour at present employed. Hitherto he had thought it wiser *not* to introduce these machines; indeed he *could* not have profitably introduced them. Now everything was different. Their introduction would therefore be begun immediately in all his factories. The wages paid would henceforth be irrespective of the work done, and the problem of unemployment would be solved in the Amusement Park!"

Mine Host was enthusiastic. But Sultan himself, who had just come from the Amusement Park, went up to bed with a heavy and a fearful heart.

The next morning he returned to the Park, to seek for the exact spot where the Palace had stood. To his surprise he found that the great heap of ashes had actually been left untouched! Only it was now used as every man's rubbish heap, broken bottles, empty tin cans and dirty pieces of paper and cardboard adding an indescribable squalor to its desolation. Indeed it was above this very spot that Abdol had chosen to erect the great hoarding that advertised his vinegar!

The sun had just set. The great Amusement Park was still comparatively empty. Not far from the Ash-Heap a man and woman busied themselves with a battered old tin box, turning it over and over between them and apparently trying to open it, until a dark-featured gentleman came up to them and offered, for a small charge, to open it with his master-key. The man and woman looked at the foreigner and then, looking at one another, winked and burst out laughing.

"Why, it doesn't matter two hoots to us whether we get it open or not!" said the man. "There's nothing in it. It's only— curiosity!" And he swore again: "—curiosity, that's all it is!" he repeated, and he kicked the tin away from him.

"Perhaps you have some old box or drawer at home that I could open for you?" suggested Sultan.

"Say," said the woman, "what particular glass case did they let *you* out of, while the museum was being hoovered? As if we ever locked anything nowadays!"

"Have you nothing at home that you value, then?"

"Stooge!" exclaimed the man disgustedly. "If we have anything valuable we take it to the Bank. Abdol keeps everything for us today—and a good job too!"

"The same answer!" murmured Sultan to himself, as he passed wearily on, "always the same answer!" Soon he reached the Ash-Heap and, leaning in the twilight on one of the rotting posts that supported the low wooden rail that ran round it, fell into a weak, unhappy reverie.

Every day now passed in the same manner. He would spend all the morning and afternoon in the Amusement Park trying in vain to earn a little money, and, when evening came, weary of his small success and indeed of everything, he would make his way to the great Ash-Heap and lean wistfully on its railings, gazing blankly at the few forlorn weeds which had found a precarious footing in this desolation, dreaming and dreaming, and wondering hopelessly what he could do. For, unless he could earn more money, it was impossible to carry out his great plan of retracing his steps back to the East, where he had intended to retire for ever into the Temple, to become a religious, and to live alone at peace.

Instead, he was obliged to go on staying with Mine Host, who for the sake of old times was accommodating him very cheaply. Ah, how he hated the Amusement Park! How the stench and the din and the dust and the vapid gigglings on every side sickened him more hideously every day! But there was something more than his disgust that made him hate it, something that made him hate and fear it, too, something which he could not understand, and which plunged him every evening when he stood, as now, by the Ash Heap, deeper and deeper into the same weak reverie. Try as he might to deceive himself, it was impossible to deny that the atmosphere with which the Amusement Park surrounded him day after day, the single-minded unending pursuit of pleasure on every side, was beginning to work on him in a subtle manner. Yes, it was arousing, deep down in his soul, all sorts of impulses, desires, hopes, all sorts of ancient greeds which until then he had believed to have been stilled for ever by one cooling touch of the constellated Virgin's wings. Do as he would, Sultan could not prevent alluring memory-visions of the old days in the seraglio, and of the debonair little concubine, from arising and floating before his eyes. It was this that troubled him most sorely of all and made him loathe, as if it were very poison, the Amusement Park and all the people in it.

It was while his mind was full of these unquiet thoughts that Sultan observed for the first time, among the sooty weeds struggling up out of the refuse on the Heap, a garden Rose. It was a sad, spindly-looking object with one dull red knob at the top, yet there was some magic in the twilight which attracted Sultan's attention to it. It was now nearly dark, and many stars had already appeared in the sky. Sultan looked at the flower again. Yes. It was *glowing!* It seemed to be giving forth a light of its own into the dusk! Or was the soft radiance that shone forth from its face no more than the diurnal gift which it had collected from the sun?

Something in the cool of the evening, and in the quiet happy glowing of the lonely Rose suddenly touched Sultan's heart and for a brief instant filled it with a peace which not even the hooting of the sirens and the momently increasing blare of the steam-organs on the roundabouts, could wholly destroy.

"I will not listen to them!" he cried determinedly. "If I have lost the hope of happiness, I have at any rate found Peace. And that is all that the wise are able to find. The rest is illusion. 'The loss of the Beloved,' said the Philosopher, 'is the finding of the Absolute.' And have I not found the Absolute? Have I not wedded the Virgin herself? Fool! What need to travel further? *I am already there!*"

As he spoke, Sultan strove with all his might to call up before his mind's eye in all its tranquil majesty, the vision of the Virgin as she had stooped to him so sweetly from the sky. But, even as he did so, two new sirens sent their long, yearning wail with an ear-splitting intensity through his temples. He put his hand to his head and shuddered to find how pale and weak, how terribly ineffectual, the image of the Virgin seemed beside the message they brought, and beside the raucous blare from all those steam-organs, and beside the smooth incessant powerful clank of all that machinery and beside the voices of the showmen calling him to pleasure, calling him to pleasure.

As if to escape the coarse, obliterating impressions of his environment, Sultan now stepped over the low railing and with his fingers in his ears walked slowly towards the centre of the Ash-Heap. It was useless; yet he refused to admit that it was so even to himself, and even as, in answer to the yearning sirens, the whole spring-tide of his shameless Eastern blood seemed to rise within him in one long starving wail after more happiness, more pleasure, after the lost luxuries of the seraglio, even in that moment, infuriated by his own uncontrollable change of temper, he shouted at the stars three pitiful and enormous lies:

"I have found the Beloved! I desire nothing! I am at Peace!" Half conscious of his dishonesty, he stooped savagely as he spoke the last word, and plucking the red rose from its little stalk, pressed it with a vindictive, almost lustful intensity, to his lips.

He started. For at the same instant he heard, close beside him, a low, mischievous laugh. It was a woman's laugh, but when he looked round, there was no woman, nor indeed any other creature to be seen. Sultan held the Rose at arm's length before his face and began gazing at it, as if it must have been the cause of his bewilderment. It was dark now over the Ash-Heap and the sky immediately above was powdered with stars, in spite of the glare thrown up by the myriad illuminations of the Amusement Park. Out of the column of darkness rising into the air above the Heap the little Rose seemed to glow at him more brightly than ever. And at last Sultan realised that it was not merely glowing but also singing to him. It was singing something like this:—

> Earth despairs not, though her Spark
>> Underground is gone—
> Roses whisper after dark
>> Secrets of the Sun.

Sultan listened to the song which as yet he only half understood, as if entranced. When it was over, he pressed the Rose once more devoutly to his lips and as he did so, bethought him, for the first time, that it would also be possible to visit the *further* side of the Ash-Heap. He immediately climbed to the top of the Heap and began to descend the other slope.

Sultan was greatly surprised to find that the other side differed considerably from the one to which he was accustomed. Instead of consisting of a single smooth slope, it was curiously scooped out, so as to leave in one place a considerable hollow. The bottom of this hollow was nearly flat, and on the side nearest the centre of the Heap rose above it in a small vertical cliff. A dilapidated old door leaned up against this side, and in the hollow, as on the rest of the great Ash-Heap, there was a good deal of debris lying about. There were some old wooden seats from a set of swings which had evidently fallen out of use, some odd straps and bits of leather, that looked as if they had to do with horses, and in the midst of all, to Sultan's great delight, one of those old-fashioned small roundabouts for children, in which the seats are wooden horses and the whole thing is worked, not by machinery, but by a man standing in the middle and turning a handle. In the Amusement Park itself this type of roundabout had long since been superseded.

Sultan began examining the debris and, in doing so, came at last to the old door. Whereupon he discovered that it was not merely leaning up against the ashen cliff as he had supposed, but actually fitted in a frame, which in its turn was built into the cliff. He tried the handle and, when he found the door locked, whipped out in an instant his little steel key. It fitted. Sultan turned the key in the lock and opened the door inwards.

He walked a long way without meeting anyone, down a winding dim-lit passage which at last opened into a huge, vaulted chamber, roughly circular in shape, in the centre of which stood a large Marquee. Sultan stopped and while he stood, looking wonderingly at the chamber, there emerged from one of the entrances of the Marquee a tall dignified man dressed in shirt-sleeves and riding-breeches and carrying under his arm a long whip. He walked without hurrying up to Sultan, and when he was within speaking distance, said to him, in a voice which, for some strange reason, filled him with happiness and made him look more closely at the speaker's handsome, bearded face, "Good evening! I wonder what I can do for you. I am afraid we have closed for the day!" Sultan enquired, not without an involuntary answering smile, what place it might be that he had blundered on, and then immediately began to apologise for intruding.

"Don't apologise!" interrupted the tall man a little more abruptly than before, and he explained that the Marquee contained a circus, and was one of the ordinary side-shows of the Fair, to which anybody was entitled to come. Sultan asked if it were much frequented.

"We hardly get a soul!" replied the tall man frankly. "The truth is, horses are gone quite out of Fashion! Indeed," he added confidentially, "we are really engaged not so much in giving actual performances as in rehearsing for a future one." He then explained that he himself was the Ringmaster and at the same time the Proprietor of the circus.

Sultan expressed his surprise that he should have chosen this particular spot for their rehearsals, since Abdol no doubt exacted an exorbitant rent. The Ringmaster smiled.

"We pay no rent!" he said. "The money does not exist, even in fancy, which Abdol would accept from us for permission to play here. Fortunately we do not require his permission. Often enough has he tried every means, both fair and foul, to evict us but, you see, Sir, I happen to have title-deeds dating back to before the Fire."

"Then it is owing to *you*," exclaimed Sultan, his eyes opening wider, "that the great Ash-Heap has been left untouched! I have you to thank!" The Ringmaster nodded, smiling again.

Sultan asked many more questions, and finally why, since the ground belonged to him, the Ringmaster had chosen to conceal his circus underground in this mysterious way. He explained that it was for safety.

"We have nothing to fear from Abdol, who cannot hurt us, much as he would like to. It is Abdol's customers of whom we have to beware. Therefore, in order that they should come one at a time, if they come at all, I had the outer door locked and arranged with Abdol himself that each person should be given a private key, as soon as he enters the Park. At present, alas, most of them lose their key before they have been in the Park five minutes. Consequently, we never see them!" Sultan informed the Ringmaster that Abdol had evidently abandoned this practice, and he himself had only contrived to get in owing to his possession of a master-key. Upon this the Ringmaster grew terribly angry.

"The old Deceiver!" he cried out and began striding up and down outside the Marquee cracking his long whip, whose loud reports echoed strangely and fiercely through the vaulted chamber, while Sultan looked down in embarrassment at the Rose which he still carried in his hand.

At last the Ringmaster became calmer, and Sultan began to enquire further about the Circus and the nature of the performance for which they were rehearsing. Before long he was asking the Ringmaster if he might join the company himself. The Ringmaster showed no surprise.

"You will begin as a clown," he said in a quiet businesslike voice. "It is the way they all begin. You will learn first of all to undress at full speed, standing; and you will sign an undertaking from this day on never to remove your clothes, together with such other garments as I shall add to them, until you can do so."

Sultan was taken aback.

"B-but," he stammered, "it will be years! I am quite a

stranger to trick-riding. I have, it is true, ridden horses bare-back but that was long ago, in Asia. We sat easily. Man and horse were as one beast. Oh Sir! I shall break my neck!" For an instant the Ringmaster was as angry as before.

"And what else are necks for?" he flashed out. Sultan delib-erated for a moment.

"I will sign!" he said at last. They went into the Marquee together.

Later, the Ringmaster showed him another underground chamber, in which were rows of wooden cubicles, in one of which he himself could sleep. Then he said good-night to Sul-tan, who thought he noticed once more an extraordinary kind-ness in his voice, and left him alone. The stables could not be far away. A muffled noise reached the cubicle of horses, mov-ing about and champing in the distance, and it was to this music that, tired out as he was, Sultan quickly fell asleep in his clothes.

When he awoke next morning, he found beside his bed a nondescript heap of old garments, which he was obliged, by his vow, to put on over those which he already wore. It was an indescribable collection. Large and small, clean and dirty (and some of them were very dirty), male and female, somehow or other he had to get them all on to his back and his disgust positively touched fainting-point, when he was obliged to draw on, last of all, and over all the rest an absurd and rather dirty pair of pink oriental women's trousers. It seemed to him that he should certainly die of shame if anyone saw him. He was there-fore greatly relieved to learn that, outside the circus tent itself, performers were allowed to wear a long black cloak, which gave them at any rate some faint resemblance to other people.

The same morning the Ringmaster took him to the stables to choose a horse. Determined to atone for the momentary weakness which had angered the master on the previous day Sultan promptly picked the largest and fieriest steed he could see, a huge black Arabian charger with a wicked eye and a magnificent stride.

This time it was the Ringmaster himself who warned him of danger.

"This kind is dangerous for the beginner!" he said. "There is too much of Abdol's strain in them! I was unable to keep it all

out. Better choose another!" But Sultan insisted on his choice
and observed with great pleasure that the Ringmaster himself
was pleased that he did so. The latter even condescended to
crack a joke with the novice, who stood holding the black horse
by the bridle and sweating under the quadruple and fantastic
burden of his motley garments.

"Room for two on that horse!" said the Ringmaster, and
Sultan fancied there was an especially friendly gleam in his
eyes as he spoke. They both laughed.

There followed for Sultan from that day, and for many a
long day afterwards, a time of hard practice. It was as rough as
it was regular. Abba, the Arab steed, did not like his new
master's looks and he frequently succeeded in throwing him,
encumbered as he was with his extraordinary burden of hetero-
geneous clothing. More than once Sultan had his bones broken
by these falls and on one occasion he lay at death's door, unconscious of everything that was going on around him, for
many days on end. The heavy jars which each of these accidents occasioned him, and the subsequent pain of his bruises
would sometimes cause him to lose all hope, even all inclina-
tion, to succeed in his undertaking and he would probably
have given up and gone away, had not the pattern of fortitude,
which he had once observed and admired in his friend the
Philosopher, come to his aid and stood him in good stead. On
the other hand, when this capacity for fortitude was itself un-
dermined by doubts of a more intellectual nature, and a certain
distrust even of the Ringmaster entered his heart, insinuating
to his despondency that there was no *reason* to continue his
pains—then the graceful figure and haunting melodies of the
Poet, with their promise of mysterious rewards, would hover
and ring in his fancy, convincing him almost against his will
that what he was doing must be worth while.

After the last serious accident, Sultan began to progress
more steadily and to gain a surer hope. For, curiously enough,
from this time on, Abba abandoned some of his most mischievous ways, as if he were convinced at last that his rider was his
master. Sultan fancied secretly that the horse had half expected
he would not have the pluck to come back after that last throw,
and that, when he found he was mistaken, he had given in.
Gradually a deep affection sprang up between man and

beast, so that they would both feel quite melancholy when night came and obliged them to part.

One night, after parting affectionately from Abba, Sultan lay on his bed, tossing restlessly in the ever increasing discomfort of his ignominious garb, itching, perspiring, and quite unable to sleep, when he felt sure he heard an impatient whinneying in the stables. "That is Abba's voice!" he cried, and the thought suddenly came to him that, being less tired than on previous nights, they might both employ a few more of the precious hours in practice. The only thing that made him hesitate was his uncertainty whether the rules of the place would allow it. He determined therefore to consult one of the more advanced performers, who had already acquired his balance and thus passed out of the clown stage—or, as they were accustomed to say in the circus vernacular, "slipped his Motley." On entering the cubicle of one of these, who was also a particular friend of his, Sultan was surprised to find it empty. He passed on to another cubicle. This, too, was unoccupied! More and more perplexed Sultan ended by trying every cubicle in the place which he knew to belong to an advanced pupil. Every single one was empty! Tired of his failures, therefore, Sultan now continued his way, without attempting to rouse any of his fellow Motleys, to the stables, where he found Abba snorting, shuffling with his feet, and pawing the ground impatiently. The horse whinneyed when he saw his master, and at once ceased shuffling. Sultan led the great black charger through the darkness of the unilluminated subterranean passages, to the vaulted chamber, which was also lampless, though a soft light glimmered through the canvas from the interior of the Marquee. He hurried towards the entrance and was surprised to find it barred by the tall figure of the Ringmaster.

"I have come for night-practice, Sir," he said. The Ringmaster shook his head, with stern disapproval.

"But," said Sultan, obstinately, his eyes on the light which glimmered through the tent, "some of the others are doing it. Why should not I?"

"*They* are not practicing," replied the Ringmaster briefly, "they are keeping the Revels!" Sultan hesitated. But the master's words only inflamed his curiosity.

"Let me just peep!" he begged in a foolish weak voice, and,

the moment he had spoken, he fancied that a change came over the Ringmaster's dark figure. Standing there with his back to the light so that Sultan could not see his face, he seemed to grow taller—to tower over the intruder with the fierce threatening gestures of an ogre.

"Back! Back!" he thundered out in a terrible voice. "Let me hear no more of it! Who sent you? *Your* time is not yet— Motley!"

Abba shivered and Sultan, too, shrank back in dismay. But before long his misery overcame his terror:

"Oh Sir!" he stammered out, "I am so tired, so tired! May not I at least take off these hideous, dripping clothes—once— just this once?" To which the Ringmaster replied in words that bit through Sultan's heart like ice:

"Yes—if you have *still* not had enough of broken vows!" Sultan slunk away abashed, leading Abba beside him, and, as he left the hollow chamber, threw one lingering look back at the soft-glimmering Marquee and at the tall figure of the Ringmaster standing dark and motionless in the doorway. Suddenly a transitory gleam lit up the master's face. Its expression was dreadful. And the arms which he had raised when he cried "Back!" and which he still held up, as if to bar the way for ever, were like two fiery serpents.

The next morning, however, the Ringmaster spoke to Sultan as if nothing at all had happened during the night. His manner was as gentle and kindly as ever, and indeed Sultan wondered how he could ever have been so much afraid of him. Later on in the day he took Sultan aside and told him that, if he really wished to continue practising by night, there was a small annexe not far from the Marquee in which he could do so. Some of the Motleys, said the Ringmaster, were already availing themselves of it. Sultan wondered why none of them had said anything to him about it.

From that time on he made use of the annexe nearly every night, though not at first for very long at a time, since he grew so quickly tired. His progress was now much more rapid, and he found himself at the same time becoming awake to much that he had formerly hardly noticed or, at best, misunderstood, in the routine and organisation of the circus. For example, there was an institution known as a Godiva-Send. Each Motley, on the day when he passed his final clown's test and threw off his clothes, became known as a "Godiva." And from time to time one of these Godivas would start out early in the morning, riding forth naked on horseback into the outside world, upon a mission whose nature Sultan still only dimly understood. Very little fuss was made over these expeditions and it was a long time before Sultan even discovered the place from which they started. He became aware much sooner of their *return* in the evening. Here the story was nearly always the same. Breathless, wounded, cruelly beaten, and covered with the excremental filth and slime which had been flung at them by crowds who had long ago become unable to bear the sight of either a horse or nakedness, they crawled back at night to the Ash-Heap and lay unconscious for many days under the tender care of the Ringmaster, who was also the Physician as well as the Leader of the troupe.

All these things, as he became more fully aware of them, began to arouse in Sultan a new curiosity about the circus and the precise object for which all this rehearsal was being conducted. He began to speak more freely about them to his companions and found that many rumours were current among them; of which, however, the most persistent was this absurd one: that it was all for fear of the electric dragons on the roundabouts in the Amusement Park!

"Why, what can there be to fear from them?" asked Sultan.

"Ah, unless they were to come alive!"

Finally Sultan summoned all his courage and actually asked the Ringmaster himself if there were any truth in this grotesque rumour. He nodded.

"What! Will the dragons really come alive, then?" And Sultan thought he detected once again a particularly friendly twinkle in the smile with which the Ringmaster looked at him, so he replied with quiet significance:—

"Everything will come alive!"

Sultan observed that, during the days immediately following a Godiva-Send, there was always a slow but steady trickle of new candidates for admission to the troupe. In this way, as time passed, their numbers swelled to an astounding degree, so that in time elaborate tunnelling operations had to be conducted, and the dimensions, both of the vaulted chamber and of the Marquee enlarged. Sultan was particularly delighted when, among the stream of new recruits, there arrived at the circus first the Philosopher and, a long time afterwards, the Poet. In the atmosphere of the circus the Poet and the Philosopher quickly gained a respect for each other which they had formerly lacked, and the three became fast friends.

The progress of the Poet was astonishing. His natural grace and dexterity stood him in good stead and his balance was so excellent that he started night-practice almost as soon as he arrived. On the other hand, he found the various restrictions which were imposed by the regulations on all members of the troupe much more irksome than either of the other two. He liked luxury, and the irritation with which he supported the incessant burden of uncomfortable and ill-fitting garments was terrible to see. Worst of all, they made him ugly and ridiculous in the eyes of his fellows! On several occasions Sultan and the Philosopher had to take him by both arms and hold him back by main force from absconding. Sultan, who felt a certain contempt on these occasions for his friend, could not escape a pang of disgust when, long before he or the Philosopher were *nearly* ready to take the test, the Poet slipped his Motley amid universal applause and joined the company of the Godivas. It was hard to understand.

As to the Philosopher, since he was thoroughly accustomed already to denying himself, he experienced none of the Poet's exquisite tortures of irritation. On the other hand his hobbledehoydom was appalling. Ride bare-back!—he could *just* about manage to sit a horse, if you first provided it with an elaborate apparatus of saddles, stirrups, blinkers, snaffles, and special leaden horseshoes to keep it from moving too fast! Moreover his congenital laziness kept him back. It was months before he would even admit that there *was* such a thing as night-practice! Moreover, he had picked a much larger and more mettlesome steed than the Poet's.

Yet even the Philosopher slipped his Motley before poor Sultan. For not only was Abba the fieriest of all the horses, but Sultan had been given a greater quantity of clothes than any of the others. He also suffered from certain hereditary physical defects, and the result of all these disadvantages was that, though quite an early arrival, he was the very last of all to pass out!

At last, however, the day came when he, too, was to be tested for his clown's diploma. The spectators' benches were crowded with fellow performers. The arena was empty. It was Sultan's day. A noise like distant thunder without the entrance and Abba comes galloping in, swallowing up the ground in front of him, snuffing it up into his fiery nostrils and gulping it down behind in a waterfall of pouring hoofs. Under his withers, clinging to the long mane in mock desperation and at the same time waving gaily to the spectators, hangs Sultan. They gallop seven times around the great arena. On the eighth round Sultan hoists himself slowly on the horse's back and sitting there as much at his ease as if he were at the chess-table passes six times more round the arena while a roar of Homeric laughter arises from the spectators at the sight of his absurd oriental trousers. Abba increases his speed. Sultan rises cautiously to his knees, to his feet, he stands on the rippling back of the rushing steed, his spine, straight as an arrow, sloping inward to the centre of the Marquee, he stands firm as the trunk of an oaktree, turning with the turning globe. At last, ah, at last, the clothes begin to be peeled off; first of all the ludicrous trousers; he kicks them neatly out of the entrance as he passes; the two pairs of tattered, worn-out boots, then more garments and yet more, until at last, upon great Abba going like the wind, his eyes fixed levelly before him in a trance that makes them seen to be both shut and open at the same time, he stands erect, naked from top to toe, waving his two arms above his head, and revelling in the glory of the cool air about his tortured skin.

There was a roar of applause as with a final turn and a wave of the hand, Sultan passed out through the entrance of the Marquee. Outside, the Ringmaster immediately came up to him, congratulated him warmly, made much of Abba and keeping an affectionate hand on the latter's mane, guided the pair to a part of the caves of which Sultan as yet knew nothing. Here, in a chamber hollowed out of the rocks below the Ash-Heap, roofed with crystal and pillared with stalactites, a hot mineral spring poured its waters with an incessant gurgling music into a natural cup or basin, which art had lipped with marble and alabaster. The Ringmaster looked significantly at Sultan.

"Take your time!" he said, "Bathe yourself and your horse at leisure. You have no further duties until to-night, when it will be your privilege, as complete Godiva, to join the Revels! And to-morrow—the dress rehearsal of your second turn!" He smiled gravely at both of them and then turned and left the cave.

Night came. Timidly, now that the hour had come, timidly and shyly, Sultan approached the great glimmering Marquee. The very nakedness, for which he had so longed, seemed to abash him, now that he had achieved it, until, at the entrance, the Ringmaster welcomed him in the friendliest manner and spoke words which made him feel at home. Sultan passed into the Marquee. It was difficult to believe that it was the same place as that in which he had so often practiced and at last triumphed. The light, by its very softness, was dim, so that to begin with, he could not see far. He observed, however, that the dry sand of the arena had been converted, by some magic, into a soft green lawn of the closest and most ancient turf. Paths led here and there to the centre, where a fountain played into a crystal basin. The surrounding tiers of wooden seats, shrouded as they were in comparative darkness, might have been an enchanted forest wherein the great arena was no more than a moonlit glade, while, scattered about the turf in an unpremeditated yet delightful confusion lay all manner of mossy couches and divans. Sultan stood entranced. As far as he could see, all the men and women whom he knew during the day as advanced members of the circus, were there, only in a slightly different form. Naked, like himself, they wandered to and fro in couples, played on the sward to the sound of music, or reposed on the divans sometimes singly, sometimes locked in one another's arms. What surprised him most of all was to see that many of those whom he knew in the daytime as elderly persons were here quite young, while some, whom he knew as young, were old and wise. Moreover the Revellers had not in every case retained their daytime sex. He saw friends mingling together as lovers, and lovers meeting and conversing as friends.

Sultan smiled to himself as he observed the Poet, a beautiful youth reclining perfectly at his ease, as if upon a couch, amid a galaxy of beautiful girls, with whom he was exchanging verses and caresses. He wondered how he himself should ever have the courage to break into one of these charmed circles, and for a long time he stood, hesitating and shy, beside the entrance of the Marquee. After a while, however, he observed, not far away from him, a figure with its back turned, standing alone. It was that of the Philosopher. Sultan had of late been thrown much together with his old friend, for whom he had come to feel a new and even deeper affection, since the latter had begun to remind him so strangely of his own father, long since dead. The Philosopher, who had not long been a Godiva, appeared, now, like Sultan himself, to be feeling shy and uncertain, and Sultan noticed that, unlike most of the others, he still looked quite elderly standing there with his shoulders bent and his head a little sunken, as he had so often stood when he came in after a hard morning in the Arena. It almost looked as if, in his case, the mysterious process of rejuvenation had not yet had time to work in him, and, seeing him thus, Sultan's heart was suddenly shaken with compassion and his eyes drenched with tears. He thought how pleasant it would be to be able to comfort the old man's weariness and restore to him his lost youth. And, behold, at the same instant a tremor passed through his limbs and he felt the light touch of silken hair about his shoulders. Looking quickly down at himself, what was his astonishment to see that the mere thought had transformed him into a mischievous fiery-eyed little brunette! He laughed merrily, and, stealing up on tiptoe behind the old man suddenly clapped his hands over his eyes. . . .

The next morning, Sultan stood alone in the arena.

"This is to be an original turn!" the Ringmaster had said to him, "you yourself will have to decide what to do!" He stood therefore alone in the arena (for even his horse had been taken away from him), waiting, and wondering if he ought to make some move, or if he should wait for circumstances to tell him what to do. Suddenly he heard the familiar thunder of hoofs— Abba's hoofs, and in a moment the dear black horse tore in through the entrance and round and round the ring. But the marvelous thing was that on his great, broad, rippling back, perfectly poised and at her ease, her long hair streaming backward, as if frozen on the wings of the wind, stood—who but the Holy One herself, the White-skinned Dancer, the Darling, the Beloved?

"Lady!" shouted Sultan exultantly in a voice louder than the thunder of the horse's hoofs and, without a moment's hesitation, summoning to his aid all the dexterity won from his painful years of practice, he leaped up beside her and hissing to Abba the single speed-word which turned his already formidable gallop into a streak of lightning, he clasped her in his arms and covered her with kisses.

After this his whole grasp of the passage of time became confused. Sometimes it seemed to him that life in the great circus was going on very much as before, and that he spent his days practising in the arena and only occasionally saw Lady, at night, for instance, when they both attended Revels. But at other times it seemed as though these same Revels were going on all the time, day and night, and that Lady was perpetually clasped in his arms, and that Abba never ceased his galloping or needed rest. Sometimes he awoke with a start to find he had been dreaming with extraordinary vividness that he had completed after all his intended journey back to the East, where he had long ago become a hermit, a man given up wholly to ecstatic visions, and Sultan even became so confused that once or twice he fancied he had never left the seraglio.

Once—or was it many times, hundreds of times?—a loud cry of

"The dragons! The dragons!"

rang through the Marquee like an alarum, whereupon Abba rushed of his own accord out of the arena, along the passage, and into the daylight. In the hollow outside they found the little wooden horses on the derelict children's roundabout on the point of turning into baby unicorns, but Sultan seized the brass rod from the back of one of them which was not yet transformed, and it immediately turned into a lance which the two of them, Lady and himself, clasped and wielded as a single warrior. They rode forthwith over the Ash-Heap out into the Amusement Park, where they found a scene of hideous confusion. The great electric dragons were one by one coming to life and proceeding promptly to devour first the human beings who had been riding on their backs and then others. Men, women, and children disappeared into the crunching, crackling jaws grinning in the most horrible convulsions of agony, while Sultan and Lady rode to and fro, selecting, wherever they could, a dragon which had not yet devoured its man and plunging, as Abba reared indignantly over the hideous monster with twitching and dilated nostrils, their lance into its gaping jaws. Behind them the half-slain dragons lay writhing on the ground, occasionally twitching in violent spasms as they spat out a crackling length of blue spark, until the little unicorns, running to and fro, finished them off with a single sharp butt of their irresistible horns.

Sultan and Lady returned to the Marquee, which immediately began to rock to and fro upon the bosom of an approaching earthquake. The ground heaved. Buildings began to fall. Fires broke out. With one terrific shock the sides of the great Ash-Heap fell apart and the Marquee rose bodily to the surface of the earth. In the midst of the Arena the tall Ringmaster stood, cracking his long whip and calling to all the company to maintain their presence of mind, and, above all, to keep their balance. Round and round the ring thundered the horses to the rhythmical crack of his whip, until slowly a curious new sound began to attract the attention of all:—

Pt! Pt! Pt! Pt!

on the roof and sides of the Marquee. Somebody went outside to investigate and, rushing in again, reported that the automatic cigarette machines had come alive and were firing off their contents at the Marquee like machine-guns. Some of them struck the canvas with such force that they penetrated to the interior, whereupon they immediately changed back into the living tobacco-plant, the paper turning into white butterflies and fluttering away while the golden colour of the weed remained hovering about the blossom in a little aureole of fragrance.

More and more of the appurtenances of the Amusement Park came to life. As soon as the automatic machines had exhausted their stock of cigarettes, they rushed madly off and began copulating with the automatic tarts, and the pornographic photographs in the stereoscopes. Once again the whole circus-troupe dashed forth and did all it could to save the miserable survivors from the appalling offspring of these obscene unions, which were growing and multiplying like gigantic lice in the warmth from the numerous conflagrations. Here all save the troupe themselves were helpless, for without horses to keep a man above the level of the omnivorous vermin, there was no hope of survival. And now, owing to the astonishing speed, power, and dexterity of Abba, none was able to do such effective rescue-work as Sultan himself. More and more of the appurtenances of the Amusement Park came alive, and even the generating stations, dotted here and there about the Park, turned into a species of colossal spider, drawing fat, black power-cables up under them like living hairy legs while the systems of light-cables turned into complicated nets in which human-beings became entangled, hanging paralysed and seeming dead, though actually conscious in every screaming nerve, until some great dynamo crawled out along its copper excrement and electrocuted them with a still stronger current.

At the end of the last nightmare, the whole troupe returned to the Marquee, where the Ringmaster commanded them sternly, whatever they heard or saw, not to leave the arena again. He had work for them now within. And, even as he spoke, a spark from one of the fires fell on the roof of the Marquee, which burst into flames, shrivelled together and soared up into the sky, while the canvas sides fell apart like the petals of a flower. The arena began to widen itself like a ripple on a stone-plashed pool. Faster and faster round it flew the horses and in the centre stood the Ringmaster, cracking his whip and shouting exhortation to the troupe. Suddenly Lady pointed up to the sky. Sultan's eyes, following her finger, rested on the crescent Moon:

"It's nearer!"

he shouted to her, astonished, above the din, and she nodded and smiled, as if nothing unexpected were happening. From beyond the circle of the arena came now the sound of catastrophe after catastrophe, with a noise as of falling cities. The whole air was full of lamentation, full of voices calling:

"Ah Woe! . . . Ah Woe! . . . Ah Woe! . . .

in slow lugubrious tones, which rose and went moaning on with a dreary insistence, so that at last there seemed to be nothing anywhere in the world but only this Ah Woe! . . . Ah Woe! . . . Ah Woe! . . . of which it was made—the great full-mouthed "Ah"s and the mournful round "O"s, until the very galloping of the horses fell into the rhythm of their alternation and the steady beat of the sighing piteous "Ah" was taken up inside the Arena by the troupe itself, resounding from their circle of sleeping-waking mouths and going up into the sky in a great enchanted yawn.

Gradually Sultan became aware that a fresh sound was in-sinuating itself, a mysterious hiss which seemed to arise out of the original sounds, and to mingle with them rhythmically, and yet also to oppose them. Where did it come from? From the Ringmaster, who was calling out slowly, regularly, again and again and again,

"Kiss! . . . Kiss! . . . Kiss! . . ."

but with such rhythmic pauses, that his voice always followed a renewed burst of wailing, so that, as the sullen ocean breaking on a long low shore moans and then sharply hisses while the waters are dragged reluctantly back over the resisting shingle, so these two opposite sounds, continually following one anoth-er, mingled together in Sultan's ears! Ah Woe! . . . Kiss! . . . Ah Woe! . . . Kiss! . . . Ah Woe! . . . Kiss! . . . rising and fall-ing, rising and falling, as if they had been going on forever. He looked at Lady significantly, too eager to obey what seemed to be a peremptory command of the Ringmaster, addressed indif-ferently to all the couples on the circling steeds. But for a mo-ment she turned her face away—and with a mocking laugh pointed again at the Moon, which hung over the Arena, by now of an enormous size and still approaching rapidly. Her face seemed to suggest that she thought the Ringmaster had been addressing, not the Earth, but the Moon. Sultan looked again. The Ringmaster stood like a tall captain upon the prow of a vessel, to which another vessel is approaching, calling calmly and sternly the orders which will bring them safely alongside. The Moon rushed down nearer. And now for the first time Sultan could perceive how the darker half of it is composed, not as he had always imagined, of rock and black shadow but

all of interweaving furious flames—clear blood-reds and brilliant Mediterranean-blues—leaping in a pursed silence, uncon-
trollably out of themselves, like the secret transports of a soul
too enraptured to speak. He turned his eyes to her and, as he
did so, the ground opened under their feet. Answering flames
shot up from beneath them. Lady returned his ardent gaze.
They burst together into floods of tears and fell to kissing one
another, and, in an instant, erect on Abba's rippling back they
had melted into one, their four lower limbs struggling downwards like intertwining roots, while their two touching breasts
strained together and upward in an endless ecstasy of desire
that was at the same time fruition. The hoofs of the horses
thundered on the flames. In the centre of the ever-widening
Arena stood the Ringmaster, grown now to gigantic stature, his
arms out-stretched above his head and forming a great cup.
Suddenly all took fire, melted into one, became a chalice of
living flames, the petals of a giant Sunflower into which the
journeying Moon fell with a long sigh of relief.

NIGHT OPERATION

"Night Operation" is more complex than it first appears. While its formal structure is imaginative fiction, science fiction in its view of a future world, it is, like *Worlds Apart* and *Unancestral Voice*, quasi-fiction in content. We are first made aware of this in the long digression (of which the narrator is mindful) on the attempt of Jon, the main character, to master the history and meaning in words. Like Burgeon, Barfield's true self in his autobiographical *This Ever Diverse Pair* (who reappears in the above mentioned books), Jon also resembles Barfield in his insatiable curiosity about—and love of—words and their meanings. The digression also reveals the evolving of Jon's consciousness as he, in his dogged research into language, arrives at a higher level of cognition and finds that words are not only expressive of man's thinking and perceiving but of life as well.

It is in the "Aboveground" experience in which Jon and his two friends share (while quite innocent of what they *see*) that the evolution of consciousness is recapitulated—*not* from the stage of original participation but from the first stage of final participation, that era of participation which is raison d'etre of Barfield's most acclaimed work, *Saving the Appearances*. In fine, we, as modern humanity, beguiled by materialism, no longer able to see the vital interrelation between seeing and feeling, between outer and inner, must relearn what has been forgotten over the centuries. It is only through the involvement of our whole being in the environment, spiritual and natural, that we step over the threshold of final participation.

The "Underground" life from which the characters take their leave is a representation of modern life, a life from which rise a few like Jon, Jak, and Peet to a "new" world already potentially in existence for those who seek it. And like them, the few must return to try to convince others still living in darkness of what awaits them—"to persuade them . . . to return to Aboveground and *live* there," as Peet tells Jon and Jak.

"Night Operation" is a contemporary allegory on the fall

129

and potential rise of humanity represented in the character of Jon, a voice crying in the wilderness of modern humanity. "Night Operation" requires of its readers what Jon learned. "There are two kinds of seeing," he tells us. "There is just 'seeing'—and there is 'being shown.'" Those who are willing to be shown will become the heralds of final participation. Though Barfield takes a dim view of modern life in "Night Operation," the piece ends on a note of hope; as the last paragraph indicates, he leaves the answer in our hands.

J. C. H.

NIGHT OPERATION

Jon began life as a perfectly ordinary baby. There was nothing to distinguish him from the hundred or so others in his creche, or for that matter from any of the thousands who were gurgling their way into humanity in the other creches of the commonwealth. As with them, it was simply that the gynaecologist's prognosis had indicated no special reason for aborting him and his mother's distaste for the messy business of child-bearing had not been quite strong enough of itself to make her opt for it. Somehow or other he had slipped in.

Like all those others he soon began, with the help of words, to construct an increasingly coherent environment out of the welter of sense-impressions wherein his consciousness at first consisted. There was the inevitable "Mam" with which he identified the nurse assigned to him—in his case, as it happened, a male nurse, since the male and female employees in the creche were exactly equal in number. Later he extended its meaning to include his physical mother, an affectionate woman who sometimes visited him. The mastery of appropriate sounds to indicate his bodily requirements and preferences came next, and these were quickly followed by a few names objective enough to begin the construction or discovery of a spatial world distinct from himself and not always friendly. Of these "floor" and "wall" were among the earliest to appear; and it was extraordinary, though not more so in his case than others, how quickly his mind began to grasp immaterial links between the names and weave them into wider unities, so that gradually he became aware of himself as a person inhabiting a place. "Floor," "walls" and "roof," for example, fairly soon combined themselves into the general term "Sewer," though a much longer time elapsed before he learned that the proper name for his particular place was "Three Forty Five" or, more fully, "Sewer No. 345"; and a still longer time before he learned to distinguish that from the even more generic term "world."

Of course the system had had to be substantially extended and deepened, but characteristically it remained sewers, and there had never been any good reason to change the name. All the less so, because the waste products they had been constructed to carry away were now disposed of in a different and less primitive way. Dehydration more or less on the spot was followed by disintegration and ended in dust.

It was the last two lessons that made the deepest impression on him. These were bracketed in the curriculum under the heading "Practical Demonstration," and were preceded by the teacher's describing to the class in simple words some of the principal features of Aboveground. As for instance that, instead of a number of different roofs, there was one very big roof called "sky"; that it was both warmed and lit by a large and very distant lamp called "sun," but not all the time. Something was said too of "stars," but Jon could make little of it—nothing at all indeed until after the Practical Demonstration. During the last two lessons the class was conducted by the teacher, at first by lift and finally up a narrow stone staircase, to a thickly glazed window or skylight above their heads, through which, one at a time, and for a few minutes only, they actually *saw* Aboveground.

Jon never forgot the sun, the more so as it was quite different from what he had imagined from his teacher's description. He had expected to see something like one of the larger non-fluorescent lamps in one of the highest roofs. But this lamp was everywhere he looked, though it was true it appeared to be especially concentrated somehow at a particular spot somewhere near one side of the window. And it was the same, when the second Demonstration followed twelve hours later, with the stars. In this case he had been unable to form any idea at all from the teacher's description. And now he was staring open-eyed and solemn, at—what? Glittering points of light that gave no light or scarcely any . . . millions of them arranged in no pattern and yet hinting patterns everywhere. When it was all over, Environmental Information was behind him and the serious business of education could begin.

In Jon's time this was based on, and developed out of, "the three Es," as they were called. And here again a digression is unavoidable. It was many years now since the long controversy over educational theory ended. It had begun with a general awareness that there were far too many different theories in vogue, many of them quite incompatible with each other, and most of them highly speculative and untested. A powerful movement arose for a return to the older and simpler practice of instructing children in "the three Rs" (reading, writing, and arithmetic) and leaving it at that. Anything else would come under some such heading as "learning" or "erudition," the encouragement of which was admittedly undesirable. The sponsors of the movement argued something like this: It is agreed on all hands that the primary purpose of education is to avert elitism by scotching discrimination. But it also has a subsidiary aim, namely the transmission of knowledge, which has been widely regarded as an end in itself. If we confine education to the three Rs, then on the one hand we achieve its primary purpose, while on the other we lean firmly on an educational principle which has been established as effective by many centuries of practice.

To this argument their opponents had two replies. First, it is not the case that instruction limited to the three Rs discourages elitism. Some children acquire them more easily and apply them more cleverly than others and in doing so become different from those others. Obsession with the three Rs belongs to the old twentieth-century ideal of equality of opportunity. Modern education aims at equality of result. Mastery of the three Rs may end in using language correctly enough to convey coherent meaning, and an ingrained habit of speaking and writing correctly is the deepest and most pernicious of all the hidden roots of class-distinction and racism. But secondly, and more importantly, that whole approach to the problem is out of date. It is based on a way of life that has long been declining and has now practically disappeared. They pointed to the actual habits of contemporary society, as evinced both in social

behaviour and in the content of contemporary art and literature. It was a travesty to pretend that these were based on a
general interest in the three Rs and what they may lead to. The
centre of attention, and thus the wellspring of development,
towards which the culture of today naturally gravitated, was no
longer the three Rs, but the three Es, that is to say, the three
excretions.

The advocates of the three Rs fought hard, but the battle
was lost almost as soon as it was begun. There might be some
room for argument about social behaviour, but as to art and
literature, it was only necessary to walk into a theatre or cinema, to watch the average TV programme, or to run the eye
down the critical columns of a weekly journal to see at once the
justification for branding the movement as reactionary. In the
end the new Education Act was passed by a comfortable majority and the champions of the three Rs were, as the ever sprightly media more than once expressed it, "dragged kicking and
screaming into the twenty-second century."

If things had gone differently, or if Jon had been born a
good many years earlier, his attention while at school would
have been directed primarily to the three Rs and secondarily to
a little of what is based on them, and he would have picked up
incidentally whatever he might come to know about the three
Es. Actually it was the other way round. His youthful attention
was directed mainly to the three excretions and their concomi-
tants and sequelae, and he picked up incidentally whatever he
came to know about the three Rs. The three Es were of course
ejaculation, defecation, and eructation. This story is about Jon
rather than about the society in which he grew up, and perhaps
the first of the accidents that led in the end to a growing diver-
gence between the two was a minor peculiarity in one of his
teachers, who was an elderly woman. Whereas the rest of the
staff spoke of fucking, shitting, and puking, she still invariably
used the longer words; and since speech-habits change slowly
and the events here recorded occurred many years after this
writing, her practice will be followed here.

Drawing his attention, as it did, to the odd circumstance
that two quite different words can be used for the same thing,
this foible of his teacher's was the first fact in Jon's experience
on which he can be said to have *pondered*. And he continued to

do so, of course only at infrequent intervals, in spite of the fact that pondering in general was not a habit that was encouraged by his elders. His thoughts on the subject are not important. In fact they were scarcely articulate enough to be *called* thoughts. They were more like feelings. What is important is that they led to his taking a difficult and very unusual initiative. An Amendment to the Education Act had retained for every pupil a certain statutory right, which an Amendment to that Amendment had considerably modified by a proviso that no public attention should be drawn to it. A teacher might or might not mention it to a pupil and, the way things had subsequently gone, if he valued his career, he generally did not. It was called "Applying for History". Briefly, it signified that a pupil whose application was accepted was given the opportunity, and some assistance, to study or at all events to receive information about what happened before the beginning of the period covered by Environmental Information.

It was Jon's teacher already referred to who decided to draw his attention to this privilege. He jumped at it, and it remained for her to forward his Application to the Principal of the School, who violently opposed it. There was a heated interview. "You must be as well aware as I am," thundered the Principal, "that it can only give the lad ideas, discriminating him from his comrades, and that *all* discrimination is democratically counterproductive." "But surely," said the teacher, "that does not mean that it is actually bad for pupils to think?"

"We cannot all think," said the Principal sternly. "But we can *all* excrete."

As however she was getting near the age of retirement, she was not afraid to stick to her guns and at last reminded the Principal that he was entitled to discourage, but not to refuse, the Application. Naturally it was only later in his life that Jon himself learned these details, and how chancy it had all been. As was the case with his physical birth, somehow or other he slipped in.

Anyway the result was that he acquired some knowledge concerning the origin of the civilisation in which he lived. Great was his surprise to discover that the sewers had been constructed for quite a different purpose than the one they now fulfilled. They had of course been constructed by the dwellers above-ground in the past, but not with any thought at all of *living* in them. They were originally used, not for human beings but for their excreta, which they first concealed and then carried away to be disposed of in various ways Jon did not trouble to follow up. This explained some of the things he had found most unsatisfactory in his life, the overcrowding for instance, which not even the panic population-control measures that followed the economic collapse had been able to prevent. But what fascinated him most was the discovery that in those days people actually *disliked* excreta and everything to do with them. And he went on to learn that it was at about the time when this dislike was already much diminished, and indeed showing signs of turning into its opposite, that two specially cogent reasons appeared for making the great change from Aboveground to Underground. Terrorist outrages were becoming so frequent in cities as to be almost a feature of daily life; and terrorism could be contained much more effectively in a literally closed society than in an open one. A still stronger motive was the chronic fear that now prevailed of a vast Airborne Invasion—not a nuclear, as had once been feared, but a bio-chemical onslaught on the life of every man, woman, and child.

The international politics of this would be matter for another story altogether. We are concerned with Jon's education. He collected the elementary information we have just imparted from scattered references in a few standard works that were shelved in the vestibule to the History Museum, under the heading: *The Discovery of Sociology.* That discovery, he also learned, could be traced back to the discovery of Real History by a fearless thinker called Darwin, and, arising from that, of Real Psychology by another fearless thinker called Freud. The discovery of Sociology (or Real Education) was in fact the third and final stage of the same progress. It was all quite interesting, and he dipped a little further into the subject of Real History, but, when he had done so, he still felt dissatisfied and in the end applied for help to an Assistant. He had so little idea of what he was looking for that it was some time before he could make himself understood; but, when he at last succeeded in doing so, "Ah," said the Assistant, "what you mean is, you would like to go on from *Real History* to *History (Ancient and Traditional)*." Jon said he supposed it was.

Once again he had to get special permission, but with the help of the benevolent teacher he managed it, and the day came when the great double doors of the Inner History Museum, or Library, were unlocked, and he found himself in a vast chamber whose walls were lined from floor to ceiling mainly with boxed microfilms, but also with many actual books of all sizes and apparently all ages. Very different from the little vestibule with its two or three shelves of up-to-date reading matter. But to Jon, to begin with, that was not its most striking feature. What filled him with awe was something else altogether. It was the silence. That not only filled him with awe but at the same time penetrated his whole being with an indescribable thrill. For it was his first experience of it.

Up to then there had never been a moment in his waking life when he was not hearing radionic music, whether or not he was hearing anything else at the same time. It is true that, during lessons in school, it was not going on actually in the classroom. The moderates in the Education wrangle had brought that about; but even before the transition to Underground, Real Psychology had conclusively established its beneficial influence on the nervous system in counteracting the human psyche's hereditary tendency to inertia. When the great transition was about to take place therefore, its experts had advised that the silence-gaps resulting from the abrupt cessation of aircraft-noise would be above danger level; and as a result the State had accepted responsibility for disseminating rock (as it was then called), at all times evenly throughout the realm. Thus, in the end, the moderates had had to agree to acoustic arrangements which ensured that, if not the detail, at least the moan and thump of it remained unceasingly audible as background. To say that Jon "expanded in the genial warmth of its absence" may perhaps convey to the reader some epigrammatic hint of the quality of the new experience. But it went deeper than that. He felt as if he was bathing in silence.

At last, however, he began to examine the books, taking them down at random from the shelves and dipping into them. It was after a day or two of this that the whole experiment nearly failed. He had so little reason for choosing one book rather than another and was able to make so little of what he did choose that he became discouraged. So much so that he had practically decided to give it all up. This, he said to himself, is the last I'll bother with, as he took down one rather large book and flung it open. He could see at once that it would be at least not *less* unintelligible than the others, and he was about to close it again, when he noticed idly that many of the Chapter-headings were single words, most of which appeared to be proper names. One of them caught his attention because the word was JOHN. Was that also a name? Was it even his own name spelt in a funny way? He ran his eye down the opening sentences and was quickly answered, for one of them stated quite definitely: "There was a man whose name was John."

The discovery seemed trifling enough, but once again it set up within him that curious process called pondering. His mind went back to his teacher's foible. Not only, it seemed, could different words mean the same thing, but the same word could become a different one by being spelt differently. How in the world had that aitch got into his name? Jon pondered. And this time he was pondering in a circumambient silence. That made all the difference. Whatever fleeting notions they were that passed through his mind during the next few minutes, the upshot of them was that he decided, before giving up, to see if it were possible to find somewhere in the Library an answer to that one question.

Anyone who has experienced library-terror—that feeling of being hopelessly overwhelmed by the sheer quantity of available books—will know that the proper remedy for it is to keep following always one particular thread of enquiry. Crystallising round that thread the liquid mass of volumes begins to select and arrange itself. Jon had stumbled on that remedy and it saved him.

It would be a hopeless task to try to follow his intellectual adventures, the blunderings, the false trails, the bleak despairs, the occasional gleams of light. He had all the time in the world. For Real Education only required three or four years, and he did not attain adult status and enter on his vocation till the age of sixteen. And after that there were still plenty of leisure hours. Somehow or other, amid almost insuperable difficulties, he followed that thread and became half acquainted with the many different realms into which it led him. There were other and still earlier forms of the name—*Joannes*, for instance. But *Joannes* was Greek, and that meant finding out what "Greek" meant in terms of Traditional History. Much reading and much time before the thread came in sight again with the discovery that *Joannes* itself was the Greek form of a Hebrew name; and that meant setting out to learn what "Hebrew" meant, again in terms of Traditional History.

Thus, his attention was constantly being diverted from the main thread of inquiry, which was the history of his own name. At the same time he never quite lost sight of his thread, with the result that everything he discovered was discovered from the point of view of words, their forms, their meanings and their histories. Actually he was not, to begin with, much interested in their meanings; but he quickly learned that, if he hoped to get anywhere, he must begin interesting himself very much in precisely that. This was because, in the books he read—even those concerned with comparatively recent history—a high proportion of the words encountered were either no longer in use in his own society or they had clearly meant to the writer something quite different from what they meant today. To progress from what an author was saying to the discovery of what he *meant* by what he was saying was Jon's first problem and soon became his principal concern. More than half his reading time was devoted to dictionaries.

A result of this was that the knowledge he acquired of Traditional History was a distinctive and in many directions a startlingly limited one. At the end for example of his excursions into Greek and Hebrew history he knew nothing about Pericles and the Battle of Marathon and very little about Moses, Abraham, and Jesus. What he had discovered was that Greek and Hebrew writers "meant" most of their words quite differently, because the Greeks felt, imagined and thought in terms of space and the Hebrews mainly in terms of time. That of course came at a late stage, but it came out of the whole *method*, which he had had perforce to develop in order to make any sense of Traditional History at all. For he quickly discovered that it was no use simply guessing at what a traditional writer meant. One had to some extent to think and feel and imagine *with* them; one had indeed to become a little different from one's ordinary self, before the key would turn in the lock. And yet the only key available was the locked door itself. It was the language they used.

Well, you had to take it slowly. You had to turn aside from the older books, even to turn aside from history itself, and begin by familiarising yourself through its literature and journalism with the mind of a fairly recent period, say a hundred or two hundred years ago. And then you could work backwards from there. The twenty-first century was no use, and the twentieth not much, because by that time the more puzzling changes had already taken place. Jon went all out therefore to saturate himself in the literature of the nineteenth century, and he never regretted it. Once you had mastered that latest meaning-shift, once you had crossed that *pons asinorum*, the way into the past, the way into Traditional and even Ancient History was not exactly a cake-walk, but at least the admittance bar across the entrance had been raised.

The language they used. The *words* they used. How to "dig" them? How to get inside them? That was the problem, that was the abiding task. At a fairly early stage he found it helpful to draw up three or four extensive lists and to make special notes on some of the items. Least difficult were the terms with an external reference. For example, although he had never encountered the words *marriage* and *family* before he entered the Library, a little reading was enough to give him a fair idea of the sort of thing they meant. And once he had mastered it, it paid substantial dividends. He saw at once how it would prove the key, when he returned to them, to any number of passages he had found quite unintelligible during his earlier spasmodic forays into the Traditional History of almost any period. And much the same was true of Ancient History. But the real teasers were the psychological, or psychologically emotive, terms. It was their affective, or *feeling content*, that so often baffled him. And it seemed to be everywhere. Even the external reference words were not wholly free from it; which meant of course that his lists overlapped. Thus, in the case of *marriage* and *family*, he had continued for some time to assume that they signified only sociological structures (although there was also the curious fact that *marriage* evidently connoted some kind of abnormal sex contract), before he was forced to detect an over-tone of feeling-meaning even in them.

They however came under the broader heading of "Words no longer in use," and this was not the most difficult list. Something must be said of it before going on to the others, but since this is a narrative and not an essay in lexicography, only a few examples will be chosen at random from some hundreds. The list included *awe, bless* and *blessing, chasten, chivalrous, condemn* (used non-legally), *conscience* (used without the conventional epithet *puritan*), *constancy, contrite, devotion, duty, gentleman, glory, infamous, lady, merry* and *mirth, patriotic, repentance, reticence, retribution, reverence, shame, temperance, valour,* and *vulgar.* Perhaps it is worth adding a little group to which he found it particularly difficult to attach any meaning at all, but in which (maybe for that reason) he took a special pleasure once he felt he had "got" them: *comely, seemly, courtesy, winsome,* and one or two others. Actually he only succeeded in "getting" them at all through an accident. Coming across the alternative spelling *curtsy,* he looked it up in a dictionary, and the description he found there, entering directly into his imagination, somehow gave him the key to the whole group.

At a more serious level he had a great deal of trouble with *honour. Honest* was still in use and seemed to promise the best approach to it. But how on earth to link the different meanings of honour the different contexts it seemed to suggest? The ordinary Oedipal guilt-complex . . . a disposition to fulfill contracts . . . a wide reputation . . . publicly emphasised admiration or acclamation . . . female continence . . . having distinguished ancestors . . . and so on. The word must have *had* a feeling-content, and it must be that content which somehow linked all the diverse meanings together. But what was it? How could he feel enough of it himself to enable understanding? How could he sufficiently participate? It was even worse with *defile.* He knew he was going to have difficulty with that one as soon as he divined that it was connected in some way with *clean* and *dirty,* both of which he had already entered in another list. Well, in the end he did really get some idea of it, and here too the reward for his pains went far beyond his expectations. For it proved to be the key to yet another word, which was itself the key to quite a large part of both Traditional and Ancient History. In fact it was his sedulous pursuit of the word *sin* that opened up for him his first narrow entry into that alien Hebrew "mindscape," where, as we have seen, he afterwards became in his own way at home.

Always it was the affective, or—to resume the obsolete term—the "feeling"-meaning, that was the stumbling-block. It was so unfamiliar. Not that the very notion of a word with feeling-content was beyond him, since there were a diminishing few still in use, *sympathy* for example, *compassion, kind, gentle, merciful, humane,* and so on, with their opposites. But then they had no other content as well to confuse him. They signified feeling, only feeling, and only one kind of feeling. One of his most formidable tasks was to familiarise himself with many other sorts of feeling, which Traditional History disclosed as having once been common property. We all have to approach the unfamiliar through the familiar and Jon was no exception. He took as his jumping-off place a certain rather queer element in contemporary usage. He had noticed for some time a whole class of words that were always used in a special way. What it was exactly was hard to say; but roughly the speaker or writer who employed them made it clear that, although he was not actually making a joke, he was not being really serious. Searching about for a class name, Jon hit on "invisible-wink words" as the nearest he could get to it. Of these he made the usual list; again it was an extensive one; and again it will be best to select only a few items. The list included *chaste, dignified, duty, holy, innocent, integrity, just, majestic, manly, moral, noble, pure, respectable, sanctity, serene, stern, sublime, upright* (psychological), *valiant, vice, virgin,* and *virtue.* The point, for Jon, was that all the words in this last category retained a faint trace of some earlier "common property" feeling-meaning and that the invisible wink indicated a residual awareness of it in the speaker.

But all this was only the coastal fringe. Behind it lay the vast hinterland of words which now had *no* feeling-meaning at all, nor any echo of one, though it had once been otherwise. Like an adventurous explorer Jon went on and on, discerning how much more widely the empire of feeling had formerly extended its bounds. But it was arduous. It was new found land, and every step he took was into the unknown. He started one of his lists, but quickly gave it up because he found it would amount to copying out half the dictionary. For the same reason we shall not in this case attempt to "short list" them ourselves, but shall merely illustrate with one particular word and its opposite the sort of difficulties he was contending with.

Gradually it became apparent to him that, throughout the whole of the period covered by Traditional History, the word *clean* had signified a great deal more than it did in the vocabulary of his own society. But what exactly *was* that meaning? To begin with all he could divine was that it was something more than "sterilised" or "antiseptic." But then the trouble was that, as he penetrated further into the interior, the something more became too much. It became too much for him to cope with. He went in fact through one of the patches of despair, when it first dawned on him that, whatever the unknown meaning might be, it would prove impossible to pack it into the definition of any one word. There had been a breath of it in almost any word that connoted approval. The same applied, in reverse, to its opposite, *dirty*. *Dirty* meant to Jon something like the condition of the floor just after the garbage pail has been knocked over. But how were you to cope with all sorts of other meanings that had once been latent in *dirty*, and still more in its archaic equivalent *unclean*? You could only get at them with the help of a whole host of further words, nearly all of which came from that other list of terms no longer in use at all. At one point he found himself making a hopeless attempt to hold them all in his mind at the same time: *filthy, foul, loathsome, disgusting, noisome, unsavoury, offensive, beastly, abominable,* and even (for his reading had by that time penetrated behind the nineteenth century) *dunghill,* and *yahoo*. It was the whiff of *abhorrence* (if that was the right word for it) in all of them that was so quaint in an age when that sort of response to anything at all except agony and death was unknown.

We have still not told the whole story of these verbal explorations. There was for instance the wondering acquaintance he made with a bunch of old "pejorative" sex words, all of them hitherto unknown to him: *carnal, fornication, incest, incontinence, lecherous, lewd, nasty, sensual,* and so forth. But too much detail grows tedious. What is much more interesting is the long-term effect it all produced in him. It has been described already how

Jon discovered at an early stage that, in order to participate enough to understand either obsolete words or obsolete meanings, he actually had to become a slightly different person. The trouble was that, as time passed and his studies continued unabated, he became a good deal more than "slightly" different from his former self. The change became so marked that it affected nearly all his stock responses and in doing so interfered with, indeed it threatened to ruin, his whole social life.

To see how this happened it will first be necessary to give some idea of what that social life was like. As the reader will expect from the account already given of educational reforms, it was "E" centred, that is to say, it was draped, so to speak, round the three excretions. At the time we are speaking of—though there were signs already of a coming change of taste—the major emphasis was on the first of the three. It mainly affected recreation, but then recreation was for nearly everyone the only leisure activity, and there was plenty of leisure. Not that there were no other games besides the various modes of ejaculation, but the excitement they offered was relatively weak and insipid. Outdoor games such as cricket and football had disappeared, when outdoors itself disappeared at the time of the move underground, and Bingo, or its successor at the time, though it was universally available, palled more quickly. Like everyone else round him, Jon was accustomed to use all three of the major modes of ejaculation: masturbation (both solitary and communal), battery friends, and live copulation. Of these only the second needs any explanation. In the second half of the twenty-first century the Electronic Tarts of a former age had been condemned by one of the women's movements as contrary to the Sex Discrimination statutes. At about the same time it was becoming clear that—as the "gay activists" of a still earlier period had once vociferously preached—the homo or heterosexual shape of the instrument was a matter of taste, irrelevant to that enjoyment of the act itself, which was what the customer was looking for. By the end of the century, technology had risen to the challenge, developing the bisexual "battery friend," with unisexual adapters, which anticipated the expected course of evolution by furnishing either sex at choice with an inflatable love-mate of either sex at choice. Removing, as it did, the tiresome problems of synchronizing orgasms,

battery friendship soon became more popular than live copulation, to which indeed it looked like dealing the death-blow.

Now even before he applied for History, Jon had largely
abandoned the third mode of ejaculation, and it was not long
before he gave up the second also. He hardly knew why, and
he was rather ashamed of his eccentricity. In reply to the re-
monstrances of his friends he could only mumble something
about "liking human beings *as* human beings," or perhaps he
would say as "persons." But so it was. It was what put him off
live copulation; and, although battery friends were not human
beings, they were so beautifully made that the second mode
reminded him too much of his *malaise* with the third. It was this
incipient tendency to detachment from social custom that
steadily, and rather alarmingly, increased with the progress of
his studies. It seemed to be developing into active distaste, and
the distaste to be expanding to cover more and more of what
was going on in his environment and even the environment
itself.

Individual and society are connected by all sorts of subtle
links that are not easily detectable; and it may have been no
accident that this very marked trend in Jon's personal development coincided with a further step that was going on in the
progress of society itself. It was no static society. It changed
with the times. General preoccupation with the first excretion
(we may call it E1) had by now been going on for a long time,
and many people, especially in the younger generation, were
getting bored with it. This in spite, or perhaps (so perverse is
human nature) even *because* of its having reached an unheard of
level of perfection. The trouble was that it had been standing
still at that level for too long. You cannot move on from perfection, and the active element in society wanted to move on. It
was therefore beginning to investigate more closely the possi-
bilities of E2. With all three of the Es, the avowed object is to
obtain the maximum enjoyment from creative production without being embarrassed or discomforted by the product.* In the

---

* It is interesting to trace the reflection of this principle in the theory and
practice of art. It was normal in Jon's time for instructors in the history of art
to teach that Real as distinct from Traditional, Aesthetic Theory dated from
the second half of the twentieth century. When the old prejudice was finally
abandoned that the aim of art was to produce something lasting, or even

case of E1, long before the advent of battery friendship, all difficulties with the product had been removed by a judicious blending of contraception with abortion, while enjoyment of the process itself had been accorded such a crescendo of medical and technological attention that it had reached what appeared to be an all-time maximum.

All the same, as the malcontents had for some time been pointing out, it was still only one *kind* of enjoyment. There were those who argued that the excitement it aroused and the special enthusiasm with which it was pursued were simply vestigial relics of an unacceptable sentimentalism which had formerly been associated with that particular excretion. They maintained on the basis of personal experience, and maintained vociferously, that, if product trouble could be handled as efficiently, there was actually more unmixed enjoyment to be had from E2 than E1. To a discerning eye changes observable for some time past in the subject-matter of hard pornography were revealing that the heyday of the penis was drawing to a close and the future lay with anality. This was the direction, they insisted, in which progress lay; the direction which, like all authentic progress, it was taking of its own accord and which it was therefore man's duty to bring about by his own efforts. It heralded moreover a new epoch of social harmony. For here was the final solution to the persistent problems arising from a felt difference between the sexes. Where there was no longer something one sex had got and the other had not, there would no longer be room for that repressed physical envy, which psychology had long ago unmasked as the hidden spring of that female antagonism which some called "feminism." By about the time Jon attained his majority, the movement was well advanced. Electronic devices for the instantaneous dehydration and dispersal of faeces, hideously expensive on their first introduction, were growing cheaper

---

"eternal," it was discovered that, *ideally*, authentic creative activity produces nothing at all. The word "happening" was invented at this time and remained in use for a few decades. Failing that, any unavoidable product must be as ephemeral as possible, so that it was sure to be blown away by the next wind of change in aesthetic fashion. (Not everyone agreed, but on the whole the better opinion was that it should in addition be qualitatively faecal.)

every few months, and it could only be a matter of time before they would be obtainable free of charge from the Department of Health and Happiness.

But before pursuing further the theme of the relation between Jon's development and that of his society, something must be said of his immediate human contacts within that society. He was, as we have seen, somewhat withdrawn and becoming more so. But he was no recluse. He had his circle of acquaintance and, what was better, two close friends. Their names were Jak and Peet. Neither of them had applied for History, but there was a triangle of affinity here, which showed itself in those shared tastes and inclinations that cannot only transcend sharp differences of opinion but may even render them interesting and fruitful instead of irritating and divisive. Such being the case, it was inevitable that about now Jon should have been spending a good deal of time on attempts at describing to the other two some of the forgotten riches he had been exhuming from the English language. Inarticulate and unsuccessful attempts they often were, but with some encouragement from the others, he persevered. Jak was the more sympathetic of the two, Peet rather inclined to jocose comment; but they both made respectful listeners. They were definitely interested. There was nickname affection, too, between the three, and before long Jak and Peet were solemnly referring to their official expert as "our English man," soon telescoped, on the analogy of words like "dustman," to "Englishman."

The best way to give some idea of the sort of thing that went on between them will be to describe one particular conversation. Jon had been recounting his appalling difficulty with the word *honour*, because of its multiple and apparently unrelated senses. Peet could make little of it and grew rather impatient.

"I don't see what all the fuss is about," he said, "What were they—distinguished ancestors, public acclamation, female celibacy, emphasised admiration (You're getting the habit of using a lot of long words, Jon!)? They obviously have nothing to do with each other. What does it matter that the same word was sometimes used for the lot of 'em?"

"I know," said Jon, "but that's just what's so fascinating! If only one could get at what lay *behind* them. There must have been some one thing behind them. Otherwise why the same word?" He paused and reflected a little. "And it's not only dead words," he added. "Take our word *love* for instance . . . "

But here Jak stopped him, stopped him with something like a sigh. "I suppose I'd better tell you both," he said. "I'd been meaning to, but I don't know . . . somehow . . . it's awkward . . . "

"What is?"

"There's been some kind of hold-up in my sex life." And he went on to tell them in a stumbling way of the curious predicament he found himself in. He had, it seemed, begun to feel strongly drawn to one particular girl. That was not in itself so very unusual. It did sometimes happen. It was the sort of thing that led to sex contracts between ageing men and nubile young women. What was bothering him, sometimes to the point of making him feel quite ill, was the fact that he didn't much want to undress or go to bed with her. "Not now anyway," he stammered out, "not for a long time . . . " no, he was not saying it would "spoil everything" . . . it was just, well, irrelevant.

There was a brief silence, which was broken by Peet. "What's it all about?" he shouted. "What's the matter with you? You'd better find a better psychiatrist. *Why* don't you want to go to bed with her? She's luscious, isn't she? Well, then!"

"Ye-es," said Jak uneasily, "she's luscious all right. But . . . " He fell silent.

Sometimes, when a friend is making an ass of himself, the best way to help him is to make a joke. Peet decided to dig Jak in the ribs. Figuratively of course, for although the thing is often said, it is in practice very rarely done. "*I* know what it is," he said with a kind of odiously allusive archness in his voice— "I believe you *honour* her!"

But Jak did not laugh. He was still thinking on from his unfinished sentence. "You see, it isn't just her three measurements and all that. *I* don't know—there's something about the way she *nods* sometimes. Something about the way she—just walks!" He began speaking more rapidly: "D'you know, you chaps, when she *smiles*—I mean, not grins, just smiles a very little bit—it's as if—it's as if—it's as if . . . all sorts of things!" he finished lamely. He turned abruptly to Jon. "There *must* have been some word for luscious that meant other things as well!" He stopped. "Well?" he added, as Jon did not at first reply . . . "Well . . . Englishman . . . what do you say?"

Jon had remained silent because he was racking his memory. "If I remember right," he slowly replied at last, "there were quite a number of them. Words are not much use without contexts to support them. But if you really want one, perhaps the one that comes as near as any to what you seem to be looking for is *winsome*."

"*Winsome*, eh?"

"Then (musingly) there was that very queer word, *lady*. It seems to have meant—." But Peet had had enough.

"I'll leave you two to go on discussing your *winsome lady* (whatever in sewers it means) by yourselves. I've got other things to do." And, with a genial wave of his hand, he turned away. Peet was more interested in changing society than in finding new ways of living in it. If he had lived in the twentieth century, he would probably have started out as a Marxist.

The other two, however, did go on discussing it for some time, and at one point even got around to *honour* again. Most of what they said was raw enough, and they felt it so.

"I'll tell you what it is," said Jak after some time sadly. "We're like infants crying in the night. We don't understand anything. We're just groping about helplessly in a world where we've never been, where no-one we know has ever been. Imagine what it would be like to be pushed out into Aboveground and told to fend for yourself! That's us. We don't know anything about the place we're trying to visit, anything about its arrangements or the life in it, anything about how to move about in it, anything about where we want to go." And, after a pause: "Jon—where *are* we going? Where is all this leading us to?"

And there was a long pause before his friend replied: "I don't know where it is leading *us to*. But I know what it is leading me *away from*."

"What's that?"

"Pretty well everything," said Jon in a troubled voice, "pretty well everything."

Mention had already been made of Jon's growing distaste for his environment. Naturally it did not make for happiness. The one tiny bit of pleasure he got from it arose from his abiding preoccupation with words; at last, for instance, he acquired an inkling of what had been meant by that forgotten word *disgusting*. All sorts of things he had formerly taken for granted began to make him feel a little sick. That might have been well enough, had they not increased so rapidly in intensity. There is no point in enumerating them, for things soon reached such a pass that it was no longer this or that but his whole world that he found "disgusting." Subjective or objective, his fault or its, the whole place nowadays—there was no other word for it— *smelt*. Of course there were still some things in it that smelt worse than others, and even of these only a few actually caused him to retch. All the same this was a reaction he could no longer always repress. Particularly so, if his occasions ever led him very close to the older parts of the walls themselves of his world. Then he *always* vomited. Their familiar smell seemed to have acquired a new quality from the knowledge he now possessed of its origin, seemed to merge, as it were, with the faintly phosphorescent radiance that shone from the thin veneer of slime on their surface, because he realised it was the residue of the waste product of a once living humanity. Nor were sight and smell the only two senses that conspired to turn his stomach. The same warmed air that wafted towards him those effluvia from the past conveyed also from the present, through gratings fixed at regular intervals in the wall, that flux of cultural diarrhoea which had once been called music, then popular music, then pop and then rock, until in the end it became too inderterminate and all-pervasive to require any name.

Here again it is interesting to note a certain parallelism between Jon's experiences and the progress of his society. We have already mentioned the trend away from E1 in favour of E2. That was widespread enough to be generally apparent. But progress is not mechanical succession. It is organic growth. Already, encapsulated within the trend, there were forming the secret stem and leaf of a further trend that would in due course blossom from it. A few eager spirits—some called them the *avant garde*—were aggressively maintaining in their little magazines that the progress about which so much fuss was being made was a hollow sham. The very fact that it was no longer frowned on by the establishment proved it. The cultural establishment, which was broadly coterminous with the media, knew very well that, when it comes to the point, E2 is not all that different from E1. It hoped, by encouraging open talk of it, to direct attention away from the really radical advance for which the age was calling, namely progress from E2 to E3.

This small but vocal section of the public made a practice of ostentatiously walking as near as possible to the old walls, in the hope of being sick. But they did not, as might have been expected, call themselves Pukers or Vomiters. In the matter of language, and especially of names for new social habits and standards, custom imposes its own inhibitions. Thus, in the nineteenth century *dentures* were "false teeth," and in the twentieth the draining and cleansing techniques proper to E1 were still referred to in polite society as "birth control." The new movement was accordingly dubbed "Nauseism" and its followers "the Nauseants." Owing to difficulties inherent in its aim, however, it soon became a complex one, with several branches. The principal difficulty was the simple fact that for most people vomiting was not at present pleasurable. Rather the reverse. And it was this that led to the first schism. One branch of Nauseism held that this reaction was vestigial only and would disappear as the technology of product-disposal improved. They referred to similar problems with E2 which were already being overcome. Their opponents however denied this, insisting that only those who accepted that it would *not* disappear were radically progressive. What the conventional Nauseants failed to realise was that the criterion of "pleasure" was itself *vieux jeu*. It had served its evolutionary purpose and was scheduled for supersession. Articles and even little books issued from their privately owned press with titles like *Pain Values, Man beyond Pleasure and Pain* and so forth. In the latest of these, *The Outgoings of Man*, the author expatiated, among other things, on the Space Travel craze which had marked the close of Aboveground civilisation. Its true significance lay, for him, not in the fact that a handful of human beings had orbited the earth for a time in receptacles of various shapes and sizes, or that another handful had fiddled about on the Moon. Nor was it scientific discovery. What *had* they discovered anyway? These might have been its conscious aims. But its true glory (he did not actually use the obsolete term) lay in the evolutionary fact that earth herself was at last beginning to excrete from her biosphere. True, that particular mutation had come to nothing. But that was simply due to the accident that space travel is incompatible with Underground civilisation. Man himself was not limited to one kind of excretion. Why then should the earth be? Other forms of telluric excretion would be discovered in due course. What form they would take we did not yet know; but one thing was certain: they would come.

It was at this point that our three friends held what amounted to a solemn consultation. It was convened by Jon, whose neurosis of repugnance had been increasing at such an alarming rate that he felt himself on the brink of a physical breakdown. He had been thinking, he told them, very hard. And he had been forced to the conclusion that there was only one course open to him, if he intended to remain sane. It would startle them. So before disclosing it he again emphasised that, which ever way he looked at it, he had found the whole logic of the situation pointing there and nowhere else. He paused, while they waited for him to say what he meant.

Then: "I must," he said, "find my way to Aboveground."

This time there was an even longer silence.

"How!" said Peet at last.

"I don't know. And that's only the first difficulty."

"What will you do, if you get there?"

"I don't know. I don't know. That's the second one. I've seen all the difficulties and dangers: how to live, what to live on, the airborne invasion—or it may even be invasions! Perhaps they are going on all the time, and we never know because we are so well protected down here. It's madness, if you like. But it's better than the other kind of madness. The question I am asking is: will you come with me?"

He had prepared himself for an even longer silence. But Jak hardly hesitated at all. In the last few months he had been more in step with Jon than Jon realised. In fact he had gone a little way ahead. He had been smelling the smell even more pungently. But he had said nothing, because he was getting used to having strong feelings and accepting them. He was not that kind of man. But now, confronted with Jon's conclusions, he at once saw the force of them and agreed to join him.

It was otherwise with Peet. He did not criticise Jon's decision, but he had impulses of his own that led in a different direction. He wanted to change things, not to turn his back on them. And he believed the time was now very near when, with a little help from men of good will, great social changes might be brought about. They already knew something of his mind, but he now disclosed what was in it more fully than he had hitherto done. He regarded the advent of Nauseism as a serious portent. Not of course what the Nauseants were saying, but the fact that they were listened to. Society's passive acceptance of unridiculed absurdities, increasing as it did every day, was a symptom that could not be overlooked. When the velocity of progress increases beyond a certain point, it becomes indistinguishable from crisis. In the pathology of serious diseases there was always a point at which progress culminated in crisis, and there followed either death, or an abatement of the fever as the first step to recovery. Peet saw contemporary society as that fevered patient. Nauseism, he argued, was a sign that society as a whole had been experiencing subconsciously what Jon had experienced all too consciously—what all three of them now experienced consciously because of the close link between them. He wanted to raise that experience to the level of consciousness in others besides themselves, in as many others as possible. How to do it? He confessed he had no plan of campaign, but added that, as far as he was concerned, he was at work on a book to be called "The Psychology of Abhorrence," or something like that. This, he believed, would at least be a step in the right direction. Up to now he had not been able to think of anything else. But if they all three put their heads together, there must surely be *something* they could do. And he ended by turning the tables on Jon and begging *them* to co-operate with *him*.

"In doing what?" asked Jon. There followed a helpless, and pretty hopeless, discussion, with Jon insisting over and over again on the need for them to *know* more than they could ever learn underground, before they could do anything at all. "We can't even see where we want to go," he said, "—because we have nothing behind our eyes." And when they asked him what he meant by that, all he could say was:

"I don't know. I don't know why I put it like that. All I do know is, that we have too much nothing in us." The argument went on for some time, but in the end Peet was won over. He made one stipulation, however. It appeared that what was chiefly worrying him was the fear that the other two might decide to stay on Aboveground. He might even be tempted himself. They *might* find life Aboveground so much pleasanter that they would forget all about Underground and never come back. That would not suit his plans at all. The others regarded the contingency as a remote one. More likely they would find it impossible even to survive up there. But they gave him all the same their solemn promise. Whatever it was like, they would all three turn back the moment they found anything of value, which it was possible to bring down with them.

II

To describe all the obstacles they had to surmount would take too long and would moreover presuppose a much fuller account of the whole society, its physical and political structures, than it has been possible to give here. Access somewhere or other to Aboveground there must be, for the simple reason that it is impossible to maintain a sewer-dwelling civilisation without it. Air for instance, however carefully filtered and conditioned, has to be admitted raw in the first place, and that alone rules out a totally closed system. They were aware therefore that some sort of connection with Aboveground was maintained by the Top Level of the Establishment. They knew also that it was sedulously guarded. But of its whereabouts, or of the personnel who controlled it, they knew nothing.

Jon, it is true, had gathered a few indications from a glance he had once bestowed on one of the more recent books in the Library. These suggested that it was the main policy of the Top Level to prevent egress. In theory anyone was free to go up. It was the inalienable right of every citizen. But in practice very very few citizens were aware of this right, and their number was decreasing every year. One of Jon's inklings was of a certain unadvertised liaison between the Department of Environment and the Department of Education. If, they now discovered, in spite of all precautions, some maverick citizen did come forward and insist on exercising his constitutional right (and the thing had been known to happen), the matter was dealt with in the following way.

The one and only port of egress was an opening in the wall behind, and very close to, an enormous building called the Personal Records Office. The way to it therefore led through that building. On entering the building and stating his purpose, the applicant was conducted along passages, which led in the right direction, but ended in a room containing a benevolent official seated behind a large desk. On the desk in front of him lay a box, which, as the official informed him, contained the applicant's "personal micro-file." He was then invited to seat himself and the conversation that ensued consisted of the official's drawing his attention to a large number of offences he had committed, or was suspected of having committed, in the course of his life, but which the authorities had not felt it necessary to pursue against him. In the main they were outwardly quite minor ones, such as income-tax evasions, sex discrimination, or unauthorised appropriations (the word "theft" was no longer in use because of its emotive overtones), but they seemed somehow to add up to a good deal. The applicant, who was amazed by both the quality and the quantity of the intimate details preserved in the State's computer bank, was then informed that, before he could exercise his right of egress, the State would be bound to exercise its own reserved right of prosecution for the offences on the file, of which those so far mentioned were examples only. It was his duty, the official continued, to add that this also applied to any transgressions not yet in the bank, but which might come to light during the prosecution. "Perhaps it will help," he would remark during the silence that followed, "if I mention that you are under no compulsion to proceed with your application. Should you, on reflection, decide to withdraw it, action of the kind we have been discussing would be considered inappropriate and the tapes destroyed, though of course the information would remain available in the bank."

In the upshot the application was invariably withdrawn. So our three friends debated whether there could be some other way. Apart from any other considerations the delays it would entail seemed to them intolerable. They might be middle-aged by the time the law had taken its interminable course and the penalties had been duly paid. Peet undertook to push an investigation. After a few days he reported that there *was* another path to egress, and one which did not involve going through the Personal Records Office. The Office abutted on the wall, but was not actually built on to it. By going round the building, instead of through it, you reached a narrow unused passage between it and the wall. But entrance to the passage was heavily guarded. Peet offered, if they agreed, to see if there was any way of circumventing or squaring the guardians, and went off with their full consent to try his luck.

The other two never knew how he managed it, whether by bribery, or by offering a short-term sex-contract to some unattractive female member of the administrative staff, or simply because of something imperious and confident in his manner of asking for things. Those who have not got this by the way are often rather ruefully surprised to observe how much it can achieve, even when entirely unsupported by any claim of right. Anyway he *did* manage it, and the day came when they threaded their way in single file over a rough floor of rubble and debris along a passage so narrow that their shoulders brushed the walls on either side, until they reached the longed-for opening, through which the way led upward. There was no door. Presumably it was considered unnecessary in view of the strongly guarded one at the entrance to the passage, which they had already passed by guile. There were flights of steps, steep sloped, then more steps and more slopes. At last however they reached a level and fairly roomy space, at the opposite end of which was the final egress to Aboveground itself.

To understand what followed it is necessary to realise that up to now in the whole course of their lives they had had almost no experience of *space*; of what we call "open" space none at all. Beyond the cave in which they were standing lay a wide stretch of open country underneath an open sky, the whole illuminated by the glow of the setting sun. But this was not what they saw. Not at first. Not for some time yet. What they saw was that one patch of a wall in front of them was luminous instead of dark and was painted with sundry unknown shapes. They knew, for after all this was the whole meaning of their quest, that it was also pervious; but they first had to *tell* themselves that they knew it. Jon passed through this stage a little more quickly than the others because of his exceptionally vivid memory of the Practical Demonstration that had come at the end of the Environmental Information class. He had already passed it by the time the three of them reached the mouth of the cave; and once there, the other two soon caught up with him.

They looked out, they looked up, and they looked down. That was simple enough. The mouth of the cave was about six feet above the level of the ground. It would be easy enough to drop down, though not quite so easy to scramble back again. It seemed a matter of course that Jon, with whom the whole expedition had originated, should be the first to go. Without much hesitation therefore he eased himself over the ledge, clung for a moment with his hands, and dropped on to the floor of Aboveground.

Here it is again necessary to emphasize that Jon had never before stood in open space. Is that enough to explain what happened next? What did happen was this. Almost instantly, it seemed, something rushed in upon him, across the world from the horizon, and down upon and round him from the sky, striding at him with seven-leagued boots from all directions, from all places except the friendly mouth of the cave he had just left behind him. It was *Fear*.

Fear. Naked and appalling terror, with no foundation. Indeed it was because he himself was suddenly without foundation that it came. No images came with it, no vague apprehension of those threatened airborne invasions, which he had always associated with Aboveground, and from which the sewer culture had hitherto protected him—although that had been one of his main anxieties in planning the expedition. It was as though he had ceased to be a thinking being and had become an embodiment of Fear itself. He turned his back on space, scrabbled with his hands on the ledge of the cave and struggled to pull himself up. But the muscles of his arms were too weak for it and it was his two friends who leaned down to him, drew him up and pulled him, open-mouthed and gasping, back beside them.

"No use," he whispered, his teeth only just not chattering, "we must give it up. We're not made for it!"

"For what?"

"For—out there!"

Jak and Peet withdrew a few paces and held a brief, low-voiced conference. Then Jak advanced to the mouth of the cave, leaned out, looked around as far as he could without dropping to the ground. And when he drew in his head, he was even paler than Jon had been, though he had nothing to say. It was Peet's turn. He pulled himself together, advanced to the mouth of the cave and without an instant's pause jumped the six feet to the ground below. He stood there for one, two, three minutes, turning to look fixedly first in one direction, then in another. Then, without haste, he turned back and with his strong arms pulled himself up and back into the cave. He was trembling a little.

"Well?" The question was shot at him by both of them.

"I—see—what—Jon—means." It was hardly as if he were uttering a sentence. He seemed to decide on each word, and then to perform the act of speaking it as a separate task. But he was dead set against going back. If they did so, after all that preparation, all that decision, they would never again have any confidence in themselves. They would be spineless, finished. The word "spineless" seemed for a moment to penetrate Jon's collapse and arouse him; but only for a moment. He remained as violently determined to give it all up as Peet was to persist.

It was deadlock between them, and they both turned to Jak as if in tacit agreement that he must decide. His therefore was the casting vote. And he wavered. He discovered in the next few moments, as he had never quite discovered before, though he had sometimes suspected it, that there were two Jaks. One of them was screaming to get away and bawling at him to vote for Jon and safety. But the other was busy with memories. It was dwelling on all they would be going back to—that hopeless world of battery friends, of everlasting dingy excretion—the whole sewer culture—the noise—the smell. His aversion from its quality was as powerful as his longing for its believed security. He remained silent for a long time, sunk in himself; but there was deadlock, it seemed, even between the two Jaks.

In the latter end a touch that looked irrelevant enough was to decide between them; it was the image of the winsome lady (which Peet had ridiculed), coming unaccountably before his mind, that tilted the balance, placed him at Peet's side and thus drew all three of them onward instead of back.

It is feared the reader may be disappointed to find in this tale very little about the outward appearance of the upper world they were now entering. If they had spent more than a few hours there, it might have been different. Much would no doubt have been said in picturesque language of nature's way of re-establishing her sovereignty over the soil of an abandoned city, the sprawling acres of wild flowers here, the heathy, humpy area beyond, pierced by the occasional pylon that had failed to collapse. Moreover they would have had time to travel, and some account must have been included of the scattered groups of men and women they would have encountered, who had continued a physically primitive existence above ground even after civilisation had disappeared beneath it. As it is, the story must be concerned mainly with their inner experiences.

Yet the distinction which that way of putting it implies had become by now a rather artificial, if not a false one. Changes had been taking place above ground as well as below, and something must be said of these before the story can proceed. They were changes in the opposite direction to those which had finally brought about the sewer-dwelling societies. Jon already knew something of these latter. For, once he had seen through, in the Library, the *fable convenue* which his education had taught him to call Real History, the subsequent direction of his studies had tended to familiarise him more and more with that long progress from Ancient through Traditional History, of which the present day and its "experiences" were the end product. Thus, although (except for that glimpse during the Practical Demonstration) he had never before seen or experienced anything natural, outside of the three Es, he knew that a certain encompassing manifold, which the nineteenth and twentieth centuries had apparently meant when they used the word *nature*, had borne a bewildering variety of other names in the course of its own long history. One of the earliest, he understood, was "gods," and he was not entirely ignorant of some other connotations of that term. But it was the progress itself of which he was principally aware. It was all mixed up in his mind with that other problem of "feeling-meaning," which had caused him so much trouble in the first place. He had begun by assuming that it was personal feelings he was trying to recover from the language of the past. Yet most of what he read seemed to suggest that, throughout much of Traditional History, either feeling or something very like it had resided about as much in nature as inside human beings themselves. And when you got back to Ancient History, the distinction between the two threatened to disappear altogether. In those days apparently people felt only what they saw—but also saw only what they felt. It must, Jon had decided, have been something like what happened in himself when he was dreaming.

Thus, it was not only that feeling-meanings had virtually disappeared from language. As the gods had long ago withdrawn from nature, so nature itself had now withdrawn from humanity. Even before the change to Underground there was left only an "outer" world, consisting almost exclusively of technologized sensations, confronted by an "inner" subjectivity unrelated to it. After it, the vestigial remains of human feeling had gradually withdrawn from the subjectivity. "Nothing behind our eyes" he had said, when they were deciding to leave, and he had added that he did not know what he meant. What he had in fact meant was his dim awareness that there was nothing behind their eyes, because there was no longer anything in front of them—and further that the two nothings were somehow one and the same nothing.

What he had no means of knowing however was that the withdrawal from it of an active mass of either empty or dirty feeling had affected Aboveground itself. A sort of cleansing had taken place, with the result that, for the few who had remained there, the divorce between seeing and feeling, and thus between outer and inner, instead of having to go on increasing, had been steadily diminishing. Aboveground was becoming a place where, if people did not feel *only* what they saw (as their forefathers had done), they certainly saw what they felt; a place therefore where any sharp distinction between seeing and vision could only be misleading. A twentieth-century reader may be somewhat disconcerted in what follows by the absence from contexts, where he is conditioned to expect them, of qualifying phrases like "as if" or "it seemed" or "they seemed to see." What he must *not* do, if he wishes to understand, is to stop at some point and ask himself: Is this a dream that is being recorded or an ordinary narrative?

Immediately the three friends found themselves together above ground, and by common unspoken consent they linked arms. It was a good thing to do. Jon felt stronger and braver, Peet felt steadier, and Jak felt he was supported on either side. Indeed—and perhaps this was another result of the changed conditions in Aboveground just referred to—it was as if a two-way current flowed through and between them: courage from one direction and wisdom from the other. The disc of the sun had now disappeared behind a haze of low cloud near the horizon, and they began walking towards the stronger light that still glowed from that quarter of the sky. There was much, wherever they turned their eyes, to look at; and both Jak and Jon would have been content to stare and wonder, not without tremors, at the strangeness of it all. It was Peet who reminded them, almost at once, that this was not enough. They had not come out on a holiday jaunt. They had a practical purpose, even if they had not yet discovered what it was. They were in business; and the first bit of that business must be to make themselves as much at home as possible in the new environment, to become *familiar* with it. That could never come of just gaping at it. Familiarity means awareness of detail. And where everything around you is new and unnamed, it means first of all *attending to* details. He made them begin by distinguishing, in the seeming chaos that surrounded them, between those shapes that were attributable to human activity of some sort and others that were not. A rusted and broken pylon was an obvious example of the former, but there were many other features that were not so simple. Was this hummock in the ground simply part of the lie of the land, or did its grassy and tangled surface conceal beneath it some stubborn human structure that had once formed part of the abandoned city? And so on. But that was not all. He made them stop from time to time to look carefully at, and then to pick, some one of the innumerable wildflowers from the straggling exuberance at their feet. It was long since vegetation had reasserted itself and covered the whole terrain in a wild profusion. Nevertheless, as Peet pointed out, amid all that variety the same particular blossom with its own particular shape could be seen recurring over and over again. He made them concentrate on one of these to begin with, until they could recognize it, when they saw it again in another place. "We haven't got a name for it," he said, "but that doesn't matter. Perhaps it's all the better. The point is, we must become able to say to ourselves: "This is *this* flower and not another." After which they went on and did the same with a few more. And so with the birds, of which there were not a few flying to and fro or busily scolding each other in the thickness of a shrub, or perched alone and singing. This was more difficult, but he was not satisfied until they had taught themselves to recognize the colours and shapes, and even the songs, of at least two or three varieties.

They had wandered perhaps a mile from their starting point when a stiff wind began blowing and the clouds spread out from the west and gradually obscured the whole of the sky. It was not long before the rain began to fall. They looked about for shelter, and fortunately the irregularities of the ground came to their aid. Soon they were ensconced under the lee of a high bank, which had sufficient overhang to keep the rain off.

They looked solemnly at one another; at first in silence; but soon they began to talk in low voices. Released from the concentration Peet had been forcing on it, Jon's mind reverted to wondering at, and pondering on, the pell-mell totality of what he had so far seen. He had occasionally tried in the past to interest the other two in the mystery of that encompassing manifold of earth and sky, once called *nature*—and before that by other names—and which in the last hour or two had become so much more real to him than mere reading had ever succeeded in making it. Its origin remained as inscrutable as the origin of his own name—or for that matter of any other name. If language and its long story meant anything, it had something to do with the *gods*—a word in which he had also on one or two previous occasions tried to interest his friends, but without much success. Now they were showing rather more interest. But there was also, as Jak pointed out, the origin of men and women to be accounted for. Hadn't that more to do with *names* than all the rest of it, and wasn't it therefore more nearly what Jon himself was chasing? What did you find out about *that* by burrowing in Traditional History? Was it from the same source? Was it first *gods*, then *nature*, then *humanity?*

Jon groped desperately, as there flitted before his mind first one or two of the little labels above the Library shelves . . . "Anthropology," "Mythology," "Religion" . . . and thena few isolated scrapings of what he had read now here and now there. At last he thought it *was*, as far at all events as the three *E*s were concerned. But apparently, in the case of men and women, there was also something else. There was, or there *had* been, something behind their eyes that came down in a different way—came somehow directly—and had never been called *nature*. He was unable to elaborate this any further. They were tired, and silence descended on them. At last Peet pronounced firmly that they must get some sleep. They stretched themselves on the ground, lying close together for warmth, and it was not long before they lost consciousness.

About five hours later Jon awoke, not through any gradations of diminishing somnolence but suddenly and totally. He sat up and looked out into the world. A moment later he rose, walked a few paces away from the bank and stood beneath the open sky. Its cloudy covering had blown across and away and, except for the eastern horizon, the stars were shining down through an atmosphere rinsed now of all opacity by the departed rain. He was not happy to be alone with them. He stepped back and aroused his friends, and soon all three of them were standing together where he had done, gazing upward in a silent communion. Now his mind could range free from the preoccupation of fear, and the first thing that entered it was a sharp memory of the second Practical Demonstration, the one and only glimpse he had had of the stars before. And how long ago that was! Moreover it had been only a narrow peep, whereas now he had the whole glimmering vault above and about him. It is difficult to describe the general impression it was making; but whatever else it was, it was not Copernican. Vast empty spaces were no part of his experience and in no way structured his imagination. It was more as if the crown of his own head had been opened and expanded and he was looking up into instead of out of it.

Mindful of Peet's discipline during the previous evening's walk, he did not let himself rest too long in the general impression, however splendid it might be. He schooled himself instead to look long and fixedly now at one patch of the profusion, now at another. The heavens, it seemed were much more difficult to pin-point than the face of the earth had been; for here were no identical repetitions to help him along, no patterns. No patterns? None, except for a few extra bright stars here and there, which he strove without much success to link together in distinguishable groups. The rest were all one faint and formless besprinkling, some of them maybe rather less faint than others. Or *were* they? If you looked again in the disciplined way, if you looked again *and* again at one patch and not another, you saw on the contrary that there were patterns everywhere, patterns too faint to be properly discerned, *potential* rather than actual patterns, inasmuch as many of the too numerous stars that went to their making were fainter than faint, too faint to make it certain that you were seeing them at all. Jon drew a long, deep breath. Was this to be the key, he momentarily wondered, to the meaning of some of those old words he had puzzled over—*gods* for instance? The other two were as absorbed in contemplation as himself. He wondered what they were thinking but had no mind to break the silence.

He had been concentrating for some time on a small patch of sky in front of and nearly above him and discerning there, to begin with, a shape like the letter *V*, with its apex pointing downwards. He did not of course know that he was looking at the little constellation of the Hyades, itself part of the greater one called Taurus, nor did it much matter. He saw only this *V* of stars, all of them faint enough, except for Aldebaran twinkling bravely at the top left hand corner. And once he had clearly distinguished it, he fixed his attention on the interior of the *V*. Was there anything there? It was not just blank sky. He could, could not, could see a plethora of fainter than faint stars filling in the interior of the *V*. Or was it rather, yes, a kind of milky veil, not made of stars at all, that had plenished it while he stared?

It was then that the monstrous happening began. The milky filling was growing more definitely opaque. Enough so for him to point it out to the other two and cause them to stare with him. Soon it was no longer simply part of the sky but standing out from it a little. But that was not the most startling thing. It was moving. Detached now from its birthplace, it was sliding along in front of the sky. Or rather it was descending. No, it was doing both at the same time. And quite suddenly they became aware that it was not alone. The same thing had been happening in many other parts of the sky; and now it was a whole crowd of these Objects that were sweeping nearer to the earth and gathering closer to each other as they did so, till there was an aerial host of them still far off and still far above the ground. But though they were as yet far away, it soon became apparent, as they dropped still lower, that they were sweeping towards the place where the three onlookers were standing. Beyond all doubt, whatever the "Objects" were, they were no part of the sky. Huge silky cupolas they seemed, with long inverted cones of pendant strands trailing below them; and they were coming nearer.

Strangers as they were to open space and innocent accordingly of any habit of long perspective vision, it did not surprise them to see the Objects growing smaller, instead of larger, as they approached. But what *were* the Objects?

"Jon! Jon! What are they?"

"Parachutes!" The word leaped into his memory out of an illustrated history book he had seen in the Library. And with it there leaped like a wild beast on all three of them the second Fear. Different in kind from the first. Then it was Nothingness they feared, but now it was something all too solid. For this must surely be the Airborne Invasion, from which they had so often been told the sewers alone protected them. Nearer and nearer came the Objects. Was this the . . .

A quarter of an hour later they were still inclined to feel that it had indeed been the End. Certainly the worst was over. They were no longer paralysed, as they had been through those long moments while they waited helplessly to learn what it was that the drifting white cupolas carried suspended so far beneath them. They were in fact seated side by side on the ground, talking together, at first in whispers and then gradually with more confidence. But everything was changed. They themselves were different people. Their tongues had been loosed, and they were speaking out of a penetration and depth of understanding they had never shown before.

The first problem was to agree on what they *had* seen after the terror lifted, as they watched the obviously harmless little spheres ("balls" Peet called them) detach themselves and roll a short distance along the ground before disappearing; while the "Parachutes" themselves rose upward and eventually faded back into the starry background whence they had curdled. Certainly the light from the sky was dim, but each felt quite sure of what he had seen. Jon insisted that the balls were golden; Peet was sure they were made of some black substance and maintained moreover that they had not sunk into the ground but had volatilized and vanished into air; Jak agreed with Jon that they had sunk into the ground, but had no doubt they were made of silver. Did this mean that none of them could have seen what really happened? That was the first question they had to settle, and it was Jon who dealt with it in his own characteristic way. "*You* ought not to be raising that question," he said to Peet, "Considering you yourself were teaching us the answer to it yesterday. Nobody sees everything. People see what they are choosing to attend to." Thereupon he recalled at some length, and not without eloquence, his long puzzling over the difference between Real History and Traditional History. Most of what they taught us in Real History, he had discovered, "is based on the curious idea that what people are not attending to is not there; and they generally go on from that to the even more curious idea (which they soon start calling the fact) that what people have ceased attending to never was there. I believe it has something to do with time—the difference between thinking *in* time and thinking *in terms* of time. But that is not the point just now. I am sure we each saw different spheres, because we were attending to different spheres. I happened to be attending to the golden ones."

Although they took some time to digest this, neither of the others raised any objection. Nor apparently had they anything to add. So Jon, speaking still more slowly now, continued his discourse.

"I am equally sure," he said, "and I think this is the really important thing for us at this moment, that seeing itself is not nearly such a simple thing as we used to assume down there. There are two kinds of seeing. There is just 'seeing'—and there is 'being shown.'"

"Ah!" exclaimed Peet, "I was coming to that myself."

"I believe," Jon continued, and at this point his tone grew slightly apologetic, "it has something to do with space—the difference between seeing *in* space and seeing *in terms of*—"

"Never mind about that!" Peet cut him sort with perhaps unnecessary haste. "The thing to do now is for each of us to tell as fully as possible just what he *did* see—or was shown. You'd better begin, because you have got going already.'

"Very well," said Jon calmly. "You know already the *skeleton* of what I saw. Like other skeletons, it had a body, and the body was alive and outside and all round it. If was much bigger and much more important than the skeleton. If you must have it, the body I saw was the beginning of the world. And now that I have seen it, it's obvious enough. I ought to have seen it long before, without having to be shown; but perhaps I made a bad start. Everything came down from the gods, and what came first of all was a name—or a word—it comes to the same thing—all words are really names. Then the other words. Then the things, as we call them. But that's not all of course. Something like it happens every time a man or woman is born. The golden balls were proper names, my own among them. Good grace! Why did I have to be shown in that crude way? It's not as if nobody else had ever seen the body round the skeleton before now. Wait till we get back and into the Library. That old picture book for instance! You know—I expect I shall be hearing from you—it's possible to see the same thing and be shown different things. But it's also possible to see different things and be shown the same thing. *I* saw parachutes dropping from the sky. They saw something quite different—or perhaps not so very different—different substance, same shape—the great inverted cone with the little morsel of Dignity at its nether tip. *They* saw a wide-winged bird flying downward and, pendant from its bill, a long loop with a new-born baby in it. *Stork* I believe they called it. Not to have seen it! Not to have understood! And yet—and yet—Jak! Peet! What is happening to us? We saw how huge they are, but not how small they can become. Could I never have gathered this little ghostly Cup into the spaces behind my eyes, if I hadn't first seen the skeleton outline of it in front of them—seen it growing smaller and smaller, as it came dreadfully nearer?"

"And now," said Peet after a slight pause, "it's my turn. As I have already said, the balls were not golden at all, but made of some black stuff, something like compressed coal-dust. I know that, because I managed to pick one up. It looked solid enough, but it had no weight and crumbled into nothing almost as soon as I touched it. So much for what one calls the 'skeleton.' As to the body of what I saw, that was very hazy. It has only filled out and grown denser and clearer, while I have been listening to Jon. Jon has always given all his attention to the past. Mine has been on the future. If he's right, that's why we saw different things. I don't think they contradict each other. Words were uttered by the gods at the start. Very well, but they have since been spoken by men, and most of them spoken very much amiss; and the things have followed them. Men call themselves 'creative' and fill a Library with books and pictures, and the world with things they have made. But in the end, for good or ill, they can only do what the gods are doing *in* them. It might have been otherwise if they had ever been fully born. As, who knows, perhaps they nearly were. And what have the gods started doing *now?* Blackballing; excreting humanity; spewing out their own creation; 'emptying the contents of the womb,' as the businesslike abortionist puts it, when he is converting a baby into excrement! Yes, Jon saw the past of humanity all right. But I saw its future. And what I saw was . . . dehydration—disintegration—dispersal—dust."

For a long time no-one spoke. At last however, "If you are right," said Jak in an even lower voice, "why were you shown?" By now the stars had disappeared from the sky, and the darkness was thinning, as it grew more and more penetrated by light from the east. The other two turned their faces to Jak to hear what he had to say.

"I needn't go on about skeletons and bodies. You know that the spheres I saw were silver. But of course, like both of you, I saw much more than that. If Jon saw what was in the beginning, and what happens again every time a human being is conceived, I know that what I saw happens every night. In Jon's language the 'body' of my vision was the 'bodies' (in the same language) of men and women now living." He stopped abruptly. "How huge they are!" he added thoughtfully, and stopped again, not thinking it necessary to tell them what lay behind that musing reflection. Or that already, while still below in the sewers, he had dimly sensed, in the case of one particular human being, the invisible presence of some vast, lightly swaying celestial superstructure, out of which she came and which was yet so much a part of her that it stayed where she stayed and moved when she moved. But he had had to pause, while there dawned on him for the first time the true nature of the obstruction that had marred his sex life. Merely to have *glimpsed* a body, he was thinking, might well induce a certain justified shyness about rushing into bed with its skeleton.

"Every night!"he continued at last. "The silver cannot stay silver. Either it will turn black, or it will change to gold. I don't know. Perhaps, when the little spheres disappeared into the earth, they were finding their way back to the skeletons to rouse them from sleep. And perhaps they were bringing down, compacted within them, something of the Beginning itself, or something at least of its tremendous energy." By this time the sun had risen above the horizon, though its disc was still hidden behind a bed of cloud. They watched, in silence, the light increasing. And then, at Peet's suggestion, they ate a portion of the food they had brought with them. Looking around them, while they did so, they noticed that a long way off a thin column of smoke was rising from the ground; and it was this that touched off a long argument about what to do next.

"There are others here," said Jon, "as I knew there must be. The next thing is to find some of them and, if they agree, to join them."

At once an entrancing vision came floating before Jak's mind of an altogether new life under the open sky, of an altogether new society, of life as it might be lived in the bosom of a quiet and loving community of authentic men and women. "Do you think," he enquired longingly, that they *will* agree? Life Aboveground would be so very different!"

"It would indeed!" said Jon, his mind on the pitiless noise and the disgusting smell. "It would indeed! Come along then! We can begin by making for the smoke." He started to his feet, and Jak, rather more slowly, followed his example. But Peet remained seated where he was.

"Wait!" he said impressively. "We can't do that. You've both forgotten your solemn promise before we started. We were to turn back the very moment we had found anything of value to bring with us. Well?"

They knew of course what that "*Well?*" meant. And so the long, and at times nearly bitter, dispute began. Certainly, Jon conceded, it could be argued that they had something of value, even of great value. But they had only been Aboveground for a few hours. He was not suggesting they should stay there for ever. But what they had seen was surely the merest beginning. There must be infinitely more here awaiting discovery. They owed it to themselves—

"Are we ready for more?" interrupted Peet. "Anyway a promise is a promise."

"Well, yes. But it all depends what we meant by 'something of value.' Besides (changing his ground completely) it might even be wrong to go back at all. How if what Jak and I saw was the past and present of the people Aboveground only, and what you saw, and saw so clearly was the fixed future of those Underground?"

Jak, who out of his great longing to see more of this wonderful Aboveground and remain there as long as possible, had been hesitating between Jon and Peet but rather inclining to the former, was here abruptly moved to intervene:

"No, No. It can't be as clear cut as that. Not yet. Not nearly." He could not forget how one dweller Underground had been transfigured for him even before last night's event. What was true of one might also be true of many others. With the memory of that event at work within him, and with Jon beside him, he felt certain he would come in time to see other people too down there as they really are. He was for keeping the promise.

With both of them now against him, Jon shifted his ground once more. But by now he was fighting a rearguard action and spoke with less conviction. Suppose they did go straight back, what difference would it make to anything? There were precisely three of them. What was it suggested they should *do?* the only thing he had heard so far was Peet's suggestion of a book on "The Psychology of Abhorrence." What if he complied and they managed to produce one? Perhaps they might. Someone had said that the easiest thing to do about anything is to write a book about it; the hard thing is to live on it. What effect would it have? He knew something about books, and he had heard of Barfield's Law of literary endeavour (when a book appears with anything upsetting in it, the few who read it don't need it, and the many who need it don't read it).

But Peet would have none of that. "Now you are calculating," he said. "That's not the point. We'll leave that to the Futurologists, please. We shall do whatever we find to do, whether it's big or little, not because we think it's likely to succeed, but because we're bound to. I don't mean compelled, I mean bound by the shape of what we've seen and by the fact that we've seen it. We shall know the direction in which our faces are turned, because there's only one way in which a face that's looked on that *could* be turned. And that's all we shall need to know. Prospects and hopes are bunk. The only reality is resolution."

"And the direction?" Jak gently enquired.

"You know as well as I do. Towards persuading, or helping others to persuade them some day or other—as many at least as are not too far gone to come—to return to Aboveground and *live* there."

At this point Jon capitulated. Completely, and not at all ungraciously. For he at once began arguing in support of Peet instead of against him. "Granted," he said, "that we can't see much ground for hope. That's not a reason for refusing to look squarely at any bit of ground we do see. There *are* those symptoms of crisis. It is a fact that more and more of them are getting sick of Underground—*literally* sick of it now—and teetering in doubt what to make of their sickness. I suppose that *could* make for open-mindedness. It might make a good many more inclined to listen to someone trying to tell them what the Airborne Invasion they're afraid of is really like. D'you know (he began to speak with greater warmth), I just don't believe it is only physical destruction they're afraid of. If it were, they would all have to be physical cowards. And damn it, they're not! I can think all too easily of at least a dozen people who are ten times braver than I am. No, they talk of Airborne Invasion, or they teach it in school, but what they're really terrified of is—Aboveground itself!"

"It's agreed then," said Jak, "that we go straight back?"

But Jon hadn't quite done with looking ahead, or with talking.

"One thing I do see," he went on. "As soon as we get back, you two will have to apply for History and come into the Library with me sometimes. Whatever we do, we must keep together. It's interesting in there, you know."

"Yes," said Peet, "and it might get much *too* interesting! Do you want us all three to get stuck in the past?"

"Well, anyway, up to now it has led us *away* from the past!"

"Still, it's dangerous."

"Yes, I know it is," said Jon. "That's why I want you there as well. You must keep me up to the mark, when I'm inclined to weaken or forget the end in the means—keep us both up to the mark. As for Jak, I see him as our Contact man—keeping us in touch with the others down there and never letting us forget the bodies round the forlorn and unsavoury skeletons."

"And what do you see our Englishman doing?" Jak enquired. But Jon was too engrossed in his thoughts to notice the interruption. "The other thing that must be done is for all three of us to get a proper license of egress. In the regulation way, through the Personal Records Office. We must be in a position to come up here again from time to time. It's true, what I said about there being so much more to discover. But, apart from that, we shall need to be refreshed."

And now it was Jon's turn to be firm. "Yes," he went on, "I've only just realized it, but that's the most important thing of all. In fact I make it a condition. If you don't agree to that, I won't agree to come back with you."

How happy he was to find that they were with him and needed no persuading. For he was thinking of the little ghostly Cup he had incautiously bared into words a while back; that it would need refilling from time to time; and that it was a vessel that could be brimmed with no other substance than its own magic Provenance awfully beheld. But then, as they rose and began to retrace their steps towards the cave mouth, a qualm fluttered in his heart of hearts. Should he never have claimed it in himself, never never never have mentioned that little Calyx of joy, however blissfully confirmed he felt it? But after all it was only to Jak and Peet that he had mentioned it; and without their presence beside him . . . he became altogether lost in wonder.

And so, as they re-enter the mouth of the cave, as they redescend the crumbling steps and the slippery slopes, as the disseminated nameless din of Underground first reaches and then grows louder and louder in their ears, and as the first faint wisps of its familiar stench are wafted into their nostrils, we have to leave them. What happened after that, how far they maintained their joint resolution, what influence they were able to exert, and what effect, if any, it had on the destiny of that closed society of sickness and the smell of sickness, from which they had momentarily emerged, is a tale that cannot be told for the sufficient reason that it is not yet known.

AFTERWORD

Anything in the nature of *comment* by me on the contents of this book would be inappropriate, since I am clearly the least capable of all people of having an objective approach. Moreover, it would involve, express or implied, a value judgment or judgments to which I am strongly disinclined. It may be however that I can supplement the biographical ingredient in the Introduction by recording two circumstances from my early life which, I have come to think, may have been in some way seminal.

In England, around 1920, a young art critic (whose name I think was Clive Bell) had written a book about the nature of art. The criterion of whether a picture or the like was, or was not, a work of art turned, he proclaimed, on whether or not it contained "significant form." That was all you could say. You must on no account enquire: "Significant of *what? Significant form* became a kind of watchword, among some aesthetes and writers on aesthetics, and very soon some literary critics raised the question whether the principle that form is everything must not also apply to the art of poetry. This led to a lot of nonsensical suggestions. Short and long lines could be arranged on the page in attractive patterns, or perhaps in colours, and so forth. I thought I detected the fallacy behind all this, and the first prose piece I ever published was an article entitled "Form in Poetry" in the *New Statesman* in August 1920, wherein I pointed out that the "form" created by poetic language exists, not on the printed page, but in the consciousness of the reader or hearer. Of course the same thing might have happened later in any event, but this was in fact the occasion of my beginning to contemplate human consciousness as a field, a category, a thing to be thought about and studied in its own right. From there the step was a relatively short one to the evolution of consciousness, which has always been my major theme.

The second circumstance—earlier in time—was of rather a different nature and may take a little longer to outline. Before the first World War, radio (or as it was then called, "wireless") was still in its experimental infancy. Neither visual images, nor even the human voice, could be transmitted, only signals in Morse code. My brother Harry, who was nearly four years older than me, was also of a more mechanical and scientific disposition (he subsequently became a doctor of science [DSC]), was deeply interested in it, and to a considerable extent I shared his interest. Together we rigged up an aerial and learned Morse code, and we often used to listen in—on our little crystal set, and of course through earphones—to a mid-day news bulletin broadcast in Morse from what was then the only available public transmission, namely a mid-day news bulletin broadcast in Morse from the Eiffel Tower.

The War came in 1914, and Harry enlisted in what is now the Royal Corps of Signals, but was then the Signals unit of the Royal Engineers. In 1917, I too reached military age, and Harry was now a wireless officer. With his help, I too enlisted in the Signal Service and by the summer of 1918 had obtained a commission and become a specially trained wireless officer, though the armistice was signed before I was sent abroad.

The point of all this is that, as part of the training process, I had had to study an elementary primer on the whole theory of electricity. It began by describing the flow of electrical current from the positive to the negative terminal of a circuit by analogy with piped water flowing from the tank or watermain to the faucet. That was simple enough, but the point came at which the primer had to reveal all sorts of differences from the analogy. For instance, the negative pole was not merely receptive, but was itself a power source. And then the return half of the "circuit" need not be a wire; the earth itself could be the conductor. And so on. I recall being puzzled and obliged to ponder.

In short, although this was nowhere expressly stated, electrical phenomena cannot be understood without introducing the concept of *polarity*. And I was being forced to become dimly aware of that fact.

The concept of polarity is not easy to define in terms of natural law, but it is easily, and necessarily, accepted as *a fact* in any context wherein electricity is involved. I cannot help thinking that this early "brush" with it may have been the reason why, later on, I was able, with the help of Coleridge, to grasp without much difficulty its decisive epistemological function. For it is so that I have perceived it. If "evolution of consciousness" has been the theme of virtually every book I have written, "polarity" is hardly less central to them. When in 1976 Shirley Sugerman initiated and edited a *Festschrift* and entitled it *Evolution of Consciousness*, it was no surprise to me that she added, as a subtitle, *Studies in Polarity*.

So much then for the prose content. There are also the poems. But if comment on the former would have been inept or inappropriate coming from its author, it would be even more so on the latter. All I can say is: They must take their chance. Which I suppose is what Horace (or was it Martial?) meant when he wrote: *Habent sua fata libelli*.

So I have only one more thing to say. Since, for chronological reasons, it is more than ordinarily uncertain whether I shall still be available when this book appears, I cannot let its manuscript go without recording how deeply touched I am by the warm interest its editors have taken in my inconspicuous little *oeuvre*, and how grateful for the surprising amount of time and trouble—trouble amounting sometimes to actual research— which they have expended in it.

NOTES TO THE POETRY

p. 23   "Translation from Petrarch"—We have used the Italian text in Francesco Petrarca, *Rime, Trionfi, E Poesi Latine*, ed. by F. Neri, G. Martellotti, E. Bianchi, N. Sapegno (Milano, Napoli: Riccardo Riccardi Editore, 1951) 226.

p. 24   "La Dame A Licorne"—Mr. Barfield confirms that he did have the great series of tapestries at Cluny in mind. Asked if it were an annunciation poem, he responded that no poem about spiritualized love can be separated from annunciation.

p. 25   "Bad Day"—A Kango hammer is a noisy, pounding machine of the period, used in construction.

p. 27   "Girl in Tube"—"Office-escape" is an analogy to the widespread gardening term "garden escape," which is a garden flower slipped into wild. "Rubber-trouble" refers to condoms.

p. 28   "A Visit to Beatrice"—Mr. Barfield tells us he wrote the first section shortly after reading *Moll Flanders* for the first time and sent it to C. S. Lewis with a suggestion that one of the Inklings send back an answer from Beatrice. Lewis wrote back that he, Barfield, should write the Beatrician response. When Barfield sent Lewis the Beatrice section, he received enthusiastic approval; but, Lewis added, the second part had rendered the first part worthless!

Barfield's continuing interest in what Charles Williams called "The Beatrician moment" and its relationship to sexual love is evidenced in his Introduction to Vladimir Solovyov's *The Meaning of Love* (Edinburgh: Floris Books, 1985): "Fortunate indeed . . . will be the bewildered adolescent who finds this golden key in his hands before it is too late, before the dead weight of common sense—*communis sensus*, the shared metaphysic of the society around him—has taught him to abandon the idle fancy of being in love and get down to the

serious business of having sex. There will be few enough of
them in any case. But then we are told on good authority that
'a single leaven leaveneth the whole lump.'"

p. 32   These two poems are on paintings in The National Gallery,
London. The authenticity of the Piero di Cosimo has been
questioned, as has the theme of the work.

p. 44   "Gender"—One of the many poems in Horatian meters (in
this case the Alcaic). These meters are of course quantitatively
and not accentually based. Mr. Barfield experimented widely
in these meters; among his papers one group of poems was
collected as "Horatian Metres." *phi* shelves = restricted library shelves for pornographic materials. Mr. Barfield conjec-
tures *phi* = fie!

p. 49   "Video Meliora"—The quote is from Ovid's Video meliora
proboque: deteriora sequor: I know the better, but I follow the
worse. *Metamorphosis*, Bk. VII, 11.20–21.

p. 53   Rust—Pelles = the "Maimed King" son of Pellam and father
of Elaine, mother of Galahad. In Malory's *Morte D'Arthur*
(Book XVII, Ch. 5).

p. 59   "Orpheus"—These passages from Barfield's master-piece are
chosen for their technical virtuosity and lyrical variety. The
play as a whole presents, in the words of its editor, John C.
Ulreich: "a fully evolved theory of myth—presented, however, not as a set of propositions about mythology, but as the
embodiment of mythic consciousness in dramatic form" (*Orpheus*, p. 136).

p. 66   "Riders on Pegasus"—These are the closing passages of a
long philosophical poem originally titled "The Mother of Pegasus" which Mr. Barfield tells us was written around 1950. In
Owen Barfield on C. S. Lewis he writes: "I ended by meditating
at some length, and ultimately writing, a sort of extension and
combination of two well-known Greek myths in such a way
that the characters and events should symbolize, at different
levels, a good many matters which I liked to think were still at
a 'pre-logical' stage in my mind . . . questions to which I did
not yet know the answers and knew that, for the purposes of
the poem, it was better that I should not know them" (p. 22).

INDEX